amazing freedom

devotions to free your spirit

and fill your heart

Patsy Clairmont • Mary Graham • Barbara Johnson

Nicole Johnson • Marilyn Meberg • Luci Swindoll

Sheila Walsh • Thelma Wells

Published by

THOMAS NELSON

Since 1798

www.thomasnelson.com

Amazing Freedom: Devotions to Free Your Spirit and Fill Your Heart

Published in Nashville, Tennessee by Thomas Nelson, Inc.

Scripture quotations are taken from the following versions: The New Century Version® (NCV). Copyright © 2005 by Thomas Nelson, Inc. Used by permission. All rights reserved. The Message (MSG), copyright © 1993. Used by permission of NavPress Publishing Group. The New King James Version® (NKJV®), copyright © 1979, 1980, 1982 Thomas Nelson, Inc. The Holy Bible, New International Version® (NIV®). Copyright © 1973, 1978, 1984 International Bible Society. Used by permission of Zondervan Bible Publishers. The Holy Bible, New Living Translation® (NLT®), copyright © 1996. Used by permission of Tyndale House Publishers, Inc., Wheaton, Illinois 60189. All rights reserved. THE NEW AMERICAN STANDARD BIBLE® (NASB®), copyright © 1960, 1962, 1963, 1968, 1971, 1972, 1973, 1975, 1977, 1995 by The Lockman Foundation. Used by permission. The King James Version of the Bible (KJV).

Cover Design: Tobias' Outerwear for Books
Interior Design: Lori Lynch, Book & Graphic Design

ISBN 10: 0-8499-0177-4
ISBN 13: 978-0-8499-0177-5

Printed in the United States of America
07 08 09 10 QW 9 8 7 6 5 4 3 2 1

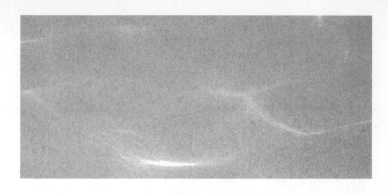

Freedom From . . .

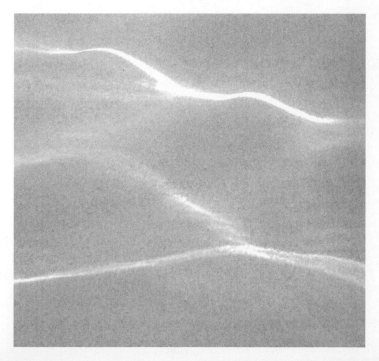

Freedom from Fear in the Storms of Life

Barbara Johnson

He calms the storm, so that its waves are still.

—Psalm 107:29 NKJV

*B*efore Hurricane Rita hit the Gulf Coast in September 2005, Veronica Alexander and her husband, Karl, along with their seventeen-year-old son, Kassel, had to make a hard decision whether to leave their home in Louisiana. "There was a mandatory evacuation order," said Veronica, who told her story to one of my friends at a Women of Faith conference last year. "But we couldn't just jump in the car and go."

Veronica's sister and brother-in-law, who lived about a half hour's drive south, had severe health problems and were not able to evacuate on their own. So Veronica and Karl hurried to pick them up. "But by the time we got them back to our home, the traffic was bumper to bumper on the road leading away from our place. It was too late to go any farther," she said. "We knew if we left we would be caught in the storm. Besides that, my husband refused to leave, and I wasn't going to leave without him."

So they made what preparations they could before the hurricane swept over their part of Louisiana. "We really didn't have time to do much. My husband took me aside and said, 'We're probably going to lose everything,'" said Veronica. "I've always teased him of being one who sees the glass half empty while I see it half full. I told him I believed God was going to keep us safe."

As the rain began and the winds picked up, Veronica walked through the rooms of her home. "I prayed, and I said that I was taking authority over this storm in the name of Jesus. I prayed for protection over our home and our family and our possessions, and then I felt completely at peace."

Her husband couldn't help but fret, however. He insisted that he had to do *something* to protect their home. "So he went outside and tied the grandkids' trampoline to a tree, even though I'd said he should just leave it," Veronica said.

That night, the family members sat inside the sixty-five-year-old, thousand-square-foot home, alternately talking about the goodness of God and watching the televised storm reports. The power finally failed about two in the morning, along with the water and phone—and all were out for two weeks.

Looking through the windows, they could see the ferocity of the storm. Meteorologists say the most destructive winds of a hurricane occur along the east wall, and that's the part of the eye that walloped their area. Then, as if the hurricane itself wasn't enough, the storm spun off several tornadoes that swirled around them as well. Outside, the world was turned upside down, and the noise was deafening. Yet inside their wood-frame home, which Veronica and Karl had renovated with eleven-inch-thick walls, there was quiet peace.

"We prayed and talked and laughed and cut up," Veronica said. "We felt completely free from fear—none of us felt any fear at all." In fact, they felt such peace they all eventually went to bed *and slept soundly as the storm blew through.*

The image of Veronica, Karl, and their loved ones sleeping peacefully in their beds brings to mind this fact from John 8:36: "If the Son sets you free, you will be free indeed" (NIV). Who else could have provided freedom from fear that night as a monster storm passed over their home? No one but the Son of God.

As if to prove just how powerful the storm had been, early the next morning when the family members awoke, they found destruction all around them. "We had to use chain saws to clear the trees out of the road leading to our home," Veronica said. "Many homes were totally destroyed—just gone. Our neighbor's brick home was heavily damaged, and the roof was blown off his barn as well. There are several metal structures in our area, and many of them were demolished. Sheets of tin were strewn everywhere."

But like an island in the middle of ocean, Karl and Veronica's home remained intact and untouched.

Oh, wait. There was *one* thing that was destroyed: the trampoline Karl had insisted on tying to the tree. "That was the only tree in our yard that blew down," Veronica said with a laugh, "and it landed on top of the trampoline. We stood on the porch and watched it happen. My husband just hung his head, and I stood there, laughing."

Now, Veronica doesn't recommend defying official orders and staying put when the authorities tell you to leave. But when you find yourself trapped in a storm with no way out—whatever kind of storm it is—she can tell you how to feel freedom from the fear that, by all accounts, *should* be part of the experience! "We prayed, and we asked God's protection," Veronica said. "We knew that whatever came, we could handle it because of our faith in him."

The faith of Veronica and her loved ones kept them going through the storm and its aftermath, when the September heat forced them out of their home and into tents as they waited for a generator—and then on the grueling, 140-mile round trip they had to make repeatedly to get fuel for the generator when it did arrive.

Veronica and her husband know their faith won't keep them out of harm's way, but they're confident it will free them from fear whenever harm confronts them.

A different storm and a different outcome confronted

Kathleen Spicer and her husband, Robert, in 2004 when Hurricane Jeanne roared through Central Florida. They, too, slept soundly that night, "knowing our lives were in God's hands," as Kathleen said. The storm wasn't predicted to pass over the town where they lived, so although there was lots of wind and thunder, they went to bed thinking they were just hearing a thunderstorm rumble through.

It seems funny now to hear how Kathleen discovered the storm had been worse than they thought. "I got up the next morning and went to make coffee like I always do," she said. "As I came into the kitchen, I noticed there was water standing on the counter—and then I took another step and realized the kitchen floor was wet."

Puzzled, she looked out the window and was shocked to see that a forty-foot-tall oak tree had blown down in their yard, and even more shocking, "the roof over our back porch was lying in our neighbor's driveway," she said.

Imagine having such peace, such freedom from fear, that you slept soundly while a hurricane ripped the roof off your home! Surely that must be the same peaceful freedom from concern claimed by the apostle Paul, who, after enduring a variety of life storms, wrote, "I have learned the secret of being content in any and every situation" (Philippians 4:12b NIV). That's a pretty strong statement, given the situations Paul endured. He was falsely accused, viciously denounced, and physically attacked before being arrested, chained, beaten, flogged, shipwrecked, and jailed for years at a time. I'll bet Paul would be one who could put his life in God's hands and sleep through a hurricane too!

What's keeping *you* awake at night? What's stealing your joy and keeping you bound by fear? Maybe you need to set your mind free from those chains that bind you to worry and torment. The prophet Isaiah praised God for keeping "in perfect peace all who trust in you, whose thoughts are fixed on you" (26:3 NLT). I want to be one of those who snore through the night in "perfect peace"!

Just think what we can accomplish when we're freed from fear and worry. One of my friends said she gained a new understanding of how we live out this kind of fear-free Christian life when she overheard her kids explaining a video game. You don't have to worry about risking your life to face the dragon or jump the chasm, her kids said, because if you play the game right, you've got another life to step into and continue the battle.

When the doctor told me that tests revealed a brain tumor that was probably malignant, he predicted, "These next twenty-four hours, as you adjust to this news, will be the hardest twenty-four hours you've ever lived."

I looked at him and smiled. *Doctor,* I thought, *you obviously know* nothing *about my life!*

At that point, God had already helped me endure enough frightening episodes to prove to me his love and support are steadfast. I'd endured having my husband Bill injured so severely in a car crash that doctors predicted he'd be in a vegetative state the rest of his life, then the death of two sons, the estrangement of another son after we argued about his homosexuality, and finally, my own diagnosis of diabetes. And after all that, the doctor thought I'd lose sleep over a brain tumor? Not likely!

God had held my hand as I'd walked through lots of fires before that one. I knew this new furnace experience probably wouldn't be easy, and it certainly wouldn't be pleasant. But I also knew that no matter what happened, I had another life waiting for me to step into. I knew the One who had created me would be with me every step of the way.

And that night, like those women who slept through the hurricanes, I closed my eyes and enjoyed a good night's sleep, free from fear.

Dear God, you walk with me through the fire and soothe my pain with your love. Thank you for giving me this extraordinary gift: freedom from fear even in frightening situations.

Freedom from
Self-Consciousness

Nicole Johnson

> Therefore I say to you, do not worry about your life, what
> you will eat or what you will drink; nor about your body,
> what you will put on. Is not life more than food and the
> body more than clothing?
>
> —Matthew 6:25 NKJV

We were on a plane traveling from Atlanta, Georgia, to Charlotte, North Carolina, on our way to a Women of Faith conference. I had flown in from Los Angeles and Mary Graham and Luci Swindoll from Dallas. We were excited to see each other, but we were not seated close enough to comfortably chat. I was about two rows behind Mary and Luci, seated in the window seat on the opposite side.

A very tall and important-looking man was sitting in the aisle seat next to me. He was already settled in when I arrived, bags in tow, coffee in one hand and cell phone in the other. He was kind and got up to let me pass by him to get to the window seat. I was beginning to get my things settled when he tapped me on the shoulder and pointed up two rows to

Freedom For . . .

contents

Mary, who was waving at me. I smiled and waved back and commented to this man that she and I hadn't seen each other in, oh, three days or so (since the last conference) and that reuniting is always an exciting event. He half smiled and went back to writing something on a pad he had in his lap. He looked vaguely familiar to me, and I was certain that I should know who he was.

Not long after we took off, he tapped me again. He pointed once again to Mary, who had gotten her coffee and wanted to show me how happy she was about this. We both enjoy coffee to an extreme and love making a big deal out of it with each other, but not usually with the man in 6B, who might be famous. He half smiled again at our silliness and kept writing.

I was working on my computer, but I was interested in what he was working on, too, as it might provide a clue to his identity. By nature I'm not a nosy person, nor do I like to read over anyone's shoulder, but I thought since we were both getting to know Mary in new ways on this flight that perhaps we should meet. "Hi, I'm Nicole," I said politely to 6B. "And that is my dear friend Mary." We both looked to Mary's seat, but she was reading the paper and not looking our way. He half smiled once more, and I asked, "What is your name?" He turned back to his writing, offering me only "Al."

I started thinking about famous Als—which is the name of a hot dog stand I know, but I didn't think this Al was he. I really thought I should know him. I decided if I could figure out why he was going to Charlotte, that would be helpful. About that time, the flight attendant came over to chat with Al. That cinched it in my mind—he was somebody all right, but I just couldn't figure out who. I would have Googled him if there had been Internet access on the airplane, but the technology to search for the identity of your seatmate while you are on the plane could be a long way off, if only because it might be considered bad form.

I was trying not to stare at him. I actually thought, *If he dozes off, it will give me a good chance to study his face.* The flight attendant asked Al why he was coming to Charlotte. Aha! My question exactly. And she had the flight manifest with the passengers' names, so she knew who he was. Hovered over my computer, I leaned in to hear Al's answer. "We are playing a date." A musician! Now my mind was racing. What kind of musician was he? "Where?" my flight attendant asked for me.

He was very cagey, this Al. At first I didn't think he was going to answer. Not that where he was playing would matter to me—I was pretty certain I couldn't go—but it would be a big clue to who this man was. "With the symphony," was his reply.

Al with the symphony. I'm not proud of this, but the symphony isn't my most knowledgeable subject. It wasn't going to shed a lot of light for me, and I found myself thinking that maybe I didn't know Al after all. Not that I really knew him anyway, but I'm sure you know what I mean.

About that time, Mary got up from her seat, presumably to use the restroom, and Al was catching on. He didn't wait for Mary to ask him to tap me on the shoulder; he just did it on his own. We both laughed, and I said hi to Mary with just my index finger in the way someone works a finger puppet.

Al and I were now friends I was sure, and I wondered if it would be polite to ask him how I might know him. I decided not. If I couldn't figure it out on my own, I didn't deserve to know. I was jealous of the flight attendant's cheat sheet, and I wondered if she hadn't had his name if she would have known. I could ask her, but I decided against that as well. What I decided to do was ask Luci when we got off the plane. She is much more up on the symphony than I am, and I was certain she would know. But Luci hadn't turned around one time during the whole flight, nor does she usually participate with Mary and me in our finger-waving antics. She's very grown up. But I knew she would know.

She did. And she was pretty much appalled by us both.

"Al Jarreau."

I started to feel the flush of embarrassment rising up my face like the mercury in a thermometer. Mary started to laugh.

Luci couldn't quite fathom how we had behaved. She looked at Mary. "You kept asking Al Jarreau to tap Nicole so you could wave at her and show her your coffee?"

That's what started me laughing. Luci was still putting the pieces together. "You two did your little finger-puppet wave in front of one of the greatest jazz musicians of our generation?" Now we hung our heads appropriately, but no matter how hard we tried, we couldn't stop the laughter. We snickered and snorted in our feeble attempts to catch our breath. (Well, I snorted; Mary doesn't snort.)

"I knew he was famous; I just couldn't place him," I offered through laughs that were quickly becoming tears from all the hilarity as the full story unfolded. Mary added, "He probably thought *you* were someone famous!" We all howled. "Um, I doubt it." More howling.

The sweet irony of this little story is that Luci is the most unself-conscious one of our bunch, while Mary and I almost always care too much what other people think. And one of the times we just let ourselves act silly, we did it in front of Al Jarreau!

I've thought of this encounter many times since, and if I were given the chance to live it over—I've decided I wouldn't change a thing. If we are free in Christ to be who we are, then I'm taking that to mean that I can do finger-puppet hellos to Mary in front of Al Jarreau and have nothing to be embarrassed about. I should be more embarrassed by all the times I've held back for fear of what someone else might think.

This time, I decided to celebrate my freedom. I gave Mary and Luci Al Jarreau CDs for Christmas.

Father, grant me the freedom to care less about what others think of me or how I appear to them and help me to care more about what you think of me and how I appear to you. Bless my days and make them full of unself-conscious moments of glorious freedom.

Freedom from a Broken Past

Sheila Walsh

God is love. . . . There is no fear in love;
but perfect love casts out fear.

—1 John 4:16, 18 NKJV

*E*ver since I was a child, I have been captivated by films, particularly drama and action movies. I am not a fan, however, of romantic comedy. The exception to that rule might be if it is a British film. For some reason, the characters and plots in the cinematic offerings from the U.K. seem more probable to me. British heroes and heroines don't always have perfect hair and gleaming white teeth, and when two such lives collide and they fall in love, I am happy for them. Most of the romantic comedies filmed in the United States star ridiculously attractive people who fall in love with other ridiculously attractive people and go on, one presumes, to produce ridiculously attractive children! I will pass.

My favorite kind of action drama is the disaster movie.

Whether it's about an earthquake, a volcano, or a fire raging out of control and threatening to consume an entire village, I am captivated by every second. I love the heroics of those who selflessly throw their bodies in harm's way to rescue a child or a three-legged dog: "I'm coming for you, Rover; hop this way!" One disaster movie in particular, released in the 1970s, topped the chart as far as I was concerned.

I was seventeen when *The Poseidon Adventure* came to my town in Scotland. It was billed as the greatest disaster movie of all time, and I could not wait to see it. On opening night, I dragged my mom and my sister, Frances, to our local movie theater. Unfortunately, I hadn't checked the starting times, so we had to sit through a very long John Wayne Western first. (In those days, movies were double billed!) It was worth it, though, as *The Poseidon Adventure* was fabulous. I walked around for days singing the theme song, "The Morning After." I had no idea then that years later I would meet Al Kasha, one of the songwriters.

From 1987 to 1992, I cohosted *The 700 Club* with Dr. Pat Robertson on the Christian Broadcasting Network. I had the opportunity to interview many fascinating people who left a mark on my heart. Some even became my friends, as is true of Al Kasha. I was excited to meet him and to tell him how much I enjoyed his contribution to one of my all-time favorite movies. His personal story, however, outshone his wonderful music.

Al was born in Brooklyn, New York. He and his brother lived in an apartment above the beauty parlor where their mom and dad worked. His father was a violent alcoholic who beat his family members every day. As a child, Al felt hopeless. Nothing he did was enough to impress his father, and his mother's paranoia brought little comfort to the two boys. She seemed to take delight in setting them up in competition against each other. Whatever one did, she would say that the other could do it better. His home was an atmosphere of discouragement and despair.

The Kashas lived across the street from the Warner Brothers studios, and as their parents often worked there as a beautician and barber, the boys had access to walk-on parts as extras. Music became the venue for Al to express himself, and it was clear to those around him that he was very gifted. After some time as a producer in New York working with legends such as Aretha Franklin and Elvis Presley, Al moved to Hollywood and began writing for films. His brother remained in New York working on Broadway. In 1972, Al received his first of two Academy Awards for writing the theme song from *The Poseidon Adventure*.

When Al got to this part of his story, I asked him what it was like for his parents to see their boy receiving that golden statue on national television. He told me that his mother said, "Perhaps one year you will be able to win a Tony Award like your brother." Al said her words pierced him to his very core. He realized that nothing he did would ever be enough. Slowly, he began to sink into a pit of despair as depression and agoraphobia covered his soul like a dense London fog. He separated from his wife, and his home became his prison.

Unable to sleep one night, Al was flipping through channels on television and stopped on a Christian broadcast. What arrested his attention was the Scripture verse on the screen, which said God's "perfect love casts out fear" (1 John 4:18 NKJV).

This seemed too good to be true. Al was Jewish, but he had many friends who had embraced Christianity, and he had watched the change in their lives. Al got down on the floor in front of the television and prayed, "If there is a Jesus, please reveal yourself." He went on to describe a great light filling his room and his heart. The following day Al and his wife, Ceil, went to church, where they both made public professions of faith in Jesus Christ.

Today, Al and Ceil still live in California. He writes and produces, but he also speaks about the difference Jesus can make in a life overwhelmed by a broken past. He said that it became clear to him that night as he knelt on the floor that not only does perfect love cast out fear, but when fear is given free rein, fear casts out love.

Fear is a ravenous beast that can eat away at our faith and paralyze us until we are unable to move. In John's first letter, he makes it clear that fear has to do with punishment, and those of us who have put our trust in Jesus don't have to be afraid of the judgment of God. He goes on to write that where God's love is, there is no fear. I believe that very truth merits some unpacking for our daily lives.

The fear that consumed Al's life before he became a believer was overwhelming. He had no control over it at all. It would stalk him, attack him, and corner him heart and soul. After Al gave his life to Christ, he still dealt with the fear that came from his broken childhood, but he didn't deal with it alone. Every time he felt the beast approaching, he was now able to invite the love of God into that dark place. So it is with you and me.

Perhaps you, too, live in the shadowy land of what-ifs or are burdened by a broken past. Whenever I find myself overwhelmed with thoughts of my past or fears about my future, I have to catch myself and get down on my knees and bring these thoughts and fears to the throne of grace. We are not guaranteed safe passage through this world, but we are promised the companionship of Christ and a peace that passes human understanding.

I don't know what kind of past you are dealing with or what fears lurk in your background, but I do know this: God is love and his love is bigger than any past circumstances or fear that would attack you.

I am learning to spend more time on my knees these days. As our world seems to spin out of control, I fall on my face before my Father and remember that he is still on the throne. I invite his love to flood every part of my wounded soul and shine light into every dark corner. Because of the love and sacrifice of Jesus, there really is a morning after!

⸻

Father, thank you for your perfect love. I invite you to flood every space in my heart and every question in my spirit with your love and peace.

Freedom from Seeking "More"

Marilyn Meberg

> Be careful! Watch out for attacks from the Devil,
> your great enemy. He prowls around like a roaring lion,
> looking for some victim to devour. Take a firm stand
> against him, and be strong in your faith.
>
> —1 Peter 5:8–9 NLT

When God lovingly created a perfect earth and placed his masterpiece, Adam, in the midst of Eden's splendor, God was pleased. But God, in his consistent concern for the well-being of his creation, thought Adam needed a companion. One of the purposes of that companion was to ensure that Adam be free from loneliness. Then Eve, in all her voluptuous beauty and perfection, was presented to Adam.

"For this cause a man shall leave his father and his mother, and cleave to his wife; and they shall become one flesh" (Genesis 2:24 NASB).

God's intention for a man and a woman was to pledge oneness to each other and no one else. That oneness was to be experienced after a healthy leaving of a mother and father and a uniting with a woman. God gave Adam the very plan God had in mind for all generations to come. Such a uniting was a freeing experience for Adam and a freeing experience for Eve. They would have each other forever. They could love each other without restraint; though naked, they knew no shame. They were utterly free. That was God's intention for them. That is still God's intention for man and woman.

Now, of course, we all know what happened to that perfect beginning. Freedom for Adam and Eve was devalued, discarded, and then destroyed forever. Why? Eve fell for the lie of the enemy, who promised more. She already had it all . . . but apparently she thought even perfection could benefit from a bit "more." I once heard Eve described as a woman with the mentality of one who repeatedly went to the post office because her computer said she had mail. But Eve wasn't necessarily dumb; she was simply greedy. Her thinking was, *Enough isn't enough; there must be more!* Rarely is there freedom for the human heart when it strives continually for "more."

This striving, this determination to have "more," often leads to a loss of freedom. How does that work? Let's look again at Eve and her loss of freedom. To begin with, she lost the confidence of her husband, Adam, who then joined her in her greed for more. She lost her home and every perfect thing God created solely for her satisfaction and pleasure.

She lost the unbroken fellowship she had with God, who strolled the garden with her and with Adam in the cool of the evening. She lost her innocence. It was only then that she and Adam both knew shame, and God made clothes for them. To be innocent is to be uncorrupted by evil, to be blameless, to be sinless. The moment she disobeyed God, Eve became one no longer sinless but one who brought upon all creation the death-producing stain of sin and its consequences.

Adam and Eve experienced a literal loss of freedom as they were expelled from their perfect home in Eden. Read these sobering words of eviction: "So the LORD God banished Adam and his wife from the Garden of Eden, and he sent Adam out to cultivate the ground from which he had been made. After banishing them from the garden, the LORD God stationed mighty angelic beings to the east of Eden. And a flaming sword flashed back and forth, guarding the way to the tree of life" (Genesis 3:23–24 NLT).

Adam and Eve are illustrations of the fact that dire consequences may accompany a loss of freedom. Often at the root of that loss is the questing for more. Had the first couple not yielded to their fascination with the possibility of more, the consequences of their decision would not have cascaded down upon them, thus evicting them from paradise.

Now let's leave the subject of Adam and Eve and their deadly contribution to society and swing back to the subject of God's intent for man and woman in marriage. God's intent is for the marriage bond to flourish and grow. The enemy, whom we first see at work in the Garden, has the opposite intent. He works against the flourishing of marriage in the hope it will die.

Scripture says that God created man and woman with the intention that they cleave to each other for the rest of their lives. I suggest the by-product of such a marital cleaving is the freedom that comes with being committed to and provided for in that union. The enemy of our souls wants always to compromise and destroy that union. One of his most frequently used tactics is to hiss in our ears, *Don't settle for this; there's more.* The unsuspecting recipient of the hiss may ask, "Where?" The response of the enemy is, *Start looking. Don't stop until you find it.* It is then the restlessness for marital "more" may begin.

How many times have you heard someone say, "There's got to be more to marriage than I'm experiencing"? How many times have you said that to yourself? I know I said it to myself repeatedly the first few years of my marriage. It was not that I had expectations of unending romance and starry-eyed dinners; I just thought it would be nice if my husband showed an interest in what I said! I would sulk and mutter to myself, "How hard would it be if you just put the paper down, looked me in the eye, and heard my words? Is that asking too much?" I was raised in a home where people's words mattered—when whoever said whatever, there was always a verbal response.

The first year Ken and I were married, I was teaching the third grade and Ken was in graduate school. My meager salary paid the rent as well as his tuition. I felt that effort alone would earn a listening ear from time to time. One evening as we sat eating our tuna casserole, I made the casual comment that the dog with rabies was back on the playground again. Ken didn't seem to hear me, so I said, "The principal was bitten as he tried to chase the dog off. It was a horrible sight, especially since the principal started foaming at the mouth this morning during our faculty meeting." Silence.

I put my head over Ken's plate and stared into his face, only a few inches from mine. I could see him trying to swallow a laugh. "Marilyn, has it come to this . . . you have to make up a story about a rabid dog and a principal foaming at the mouth to get my attention?" Soberly I said, "I've been reduced to wild storytelling, and it's your fault. Who knows what I may say to someone who is actually listening to me?"

Our laughter eased the tension, but it didn't cure the problem. Ken and I had work to do on our communication. Fortunately, he was able to see his patterns of inattentiveness and was open to hearing me say what it felt like to have my words fall on the floor after first bouncing off his face.

Communication problems are one of the major reasons for a spouse to think, *Maybe there's more.* How easy it was for me to think, *Maybe there's someone out there who will hang on my every utterance and, when I become silent, beg me to talk more.*

I would have lost freedom by yielding to the hiss, *There's more, Marilyn. There's someone out there who will be charmed by your words.* I believe I would have lost the inner sense of freedom that accompanies knowing I am being obedient to God. I am told to honor my marriage vow and to cleave to my husband. When we are disobedient to God's intent for us, we feel guilty. Feeling guilty and feeling free don't sit well together.

Now, I realize a husband whose major vice is poor listening skills is nothing compared to what many of you may be experiencing in terms of marital strife. Those of you who know my peppery nature are aware I never advise that you cleave to your husband doggedly when there's infidelity or physical abuse for you and your children. A man who subjects his wife and children to such ungodly behavior deserves to find himself alone.

This devotion then is meant to address not the abused woman but the woman who, like Eve, has most of her needs met but is easily distracted by the promise of more. I suggest to that woman, be careful. You're on the verge of losing your freedom if you follow the hiss of the enemy.

First Peter 5 warns us, "Be careful! Watch out for attacks from the Devil, your great enemy. He prowls around like a roaring lion, looking for some victim to devour. Take a firm stand against him, and be strong in your faith" (vv. 8–9 NLT).

What if Eve had stood firm in her faith? What if she had realized old "Liver Lips" was trying to talk her into disobeying the only Father she had ever known? What if she had chosen to cleave to her husband and, in commitment to their oneness, refused to even consider an offer of some forbidden "more"? What if she'd turned and walked away, leaving Liver Lips to choke on the dust of his lies and deceit?

If she had, you and I would live in a world where Nordstrom would have nothing to offer us innocent Eden dwellers.

Dear God, help me not to give in to the enemy's hiss telling me that I should look for something more. Instead, enable me to experience the freedom that comes in being content with what you have given me.

Freedom from Worry

Thelma Wells

You will keep him in perfect peace,
Whose mind is stayed on You,
Because he trusts in You.

—Isaiah 26:3 NKJV

After planning my own steps for December 2005 and the following year, I discovered God had another plan. His route for my journey was not to run around like a chicken with my head cut off during the Christmas holidays, not to travel as I had prepared, not to socialize as I had desired, and not to work as I wanted to—but to totally rest and rely on him. So instead of following through on all my well-intentioned plans, I found myself with a sickness that confined me to bed.

How easily we forget that God is really in control of everything. How arrogant of us to think we are running anything!

My sickness did not worry me one bit. No, it was lying in bed that got on my last nerve. It was depending on other people for everything I needed. It was the humiliating experience of not being able to do things for myself that I'd done for other people all my life. My worry was that I was not any service to anybody, not even to myself.

Some days I would lie there and cry. Some days I'd get angry with myself for being sick. Some days I'd take chances and try to do for myself, always failing at the pity-party bit and taking actions to prove I was okay. I'd never classified myself as a worrywart. I've heard it said that approximately 75 percent of the things we worry about never happen and at least 23 percent of the things we worry about are things we don't have control over anyway. Only an extremely small amount of the things we worry about actually take place, and worrying about them doesn't make a difference anyway.

After my eyes were opened to the fact that God is in control (and I'm not), I started on my way to excellence by not worrying. As the song says, "Don't worry. Be happy!"

This is the day that the Lord has made. We will rejoice and be glad in each of our 365 days a year. We are to live one day at a time . . . so forget about yesterday, and don't worry about tomorrow.

This year, my plan is to stay in the perfect will of God, according to Romans 12:1–2. I like how those verses are paraphrased in *The Message* Bible: "So here's what I want you to do, God helping you: Take your everyday, ordinary life— your sleeping, eating, going-to-work, and walking-around life—and place it before God as an offering. Embracing what God does for you is the best thing you can do for him."

My "walking-around" life has been full for all my over-sixty years. I've had an eventful and enjoyable life despite some of the anguish I've experienced. Perhaps because my life has been so full and favorable, I tend to forget that I have little control over anything that happens to me. Sure, I have the privilege to make choices and those choices help determine my outcome or consequences, but let's face it, nothing can happen to us without God knowing about it and allowing it to happen. Remember, he is in control! His mercies fail not. His truth endures forever. He gives more grace than we deserve. He cares for us better than he cares for the lilies of the fields.

Then why did I fall into the worry trap? I must have forgotten who's really taking care of me. Silly girl! I'm convinced that worry happens when you attempt to chart your own course. In my opinion, we are all control freaks. I've even heard people say that God helps those who help themselves. There is absolutely no biblical support for this common but self-infested cliché. Or people say that God gave us a brain to use, and if we're not going to use it, why should we expect him to think for us? This statement is totally ludicrous. (We can say some of the weirdest things!) Without the help of the Master, I could not think, speak, touch, feel, or talk. For the facts about worrying, all we have to do is go to the Bible.

In Romans 12:1–2, we are told to submit our bodies as a living sacrifice totally acceptable to God. We are to sacrifice our untamed, limited thinking to the God who made our brains and our senses. It's a sacrifice because we want to think we're in control. We want to think that we can change people, circumstances, and things. We want to think we are empowered with our intellect and know-how and that people think so much of us that they will do what we want them to do. We want to think we can orchestrate changes on our own. Yet we cannot even breathe on our own without the breath of God being in us and his hands holding the atmosphere together and expending oxygen to us in a form we cannot even see. Come on, now. Who are we fooling? We are not really controlling anything!

When I need a "stop worrying" fix, I go to the Scripture:

- "[Cast] all your care upon Him, for He cares for you" (1 Peter 5:7 NKJV).
- "Let not your heart be troubled; you believe in God, believe also in Me" (John 14:1 NKJV).
- "Be anxious for nothing, but in everything by prayer and supplication, with thanksgiving, let your requests be made known to God; and the peace of God, which surpasses all understanding, will guard your hearts and minds through Christ Jesus" (Philippians 4:6–7 NKJV).

- "Let the peace of God rule in your hearts, to which also you were called in one body; and be thankful" (Colossians 3:15 NKJV).
- "I will both lie down in peace, and sleep; For You alone, O LORD, make me dwell in safety" (Psalm 4:8 NKJV).
- "When you lie down, you will not be afraid; yes, you will lie down and your sleep will be sweet" (Proverbs 3:24 NKJV).
- "My God shall supply all your need according to His riches in glory by Christ Jesus" (Philippians 4:19 NKJV).
- "Peace I leave with you, My peace I give to you; not as the world gives do I give to you. Let not your heart be troubled, neither let it be afraid" (John 14:27 NKJV).

When I think about the opportunity to live more freely and abundantly this year than last year, I marvel that God would give me another chance—and I'm excited about it too. That means another chance to include more rest and relaxation, to choose my foods wisely, to work more productively, to adjust my activities, and to use my time more efficiently as I allow God to orchestrate my life. These are not resolutions. These are lifestyle realignments that will take me through a lifetime of expecting excellent results.

Are you willing to join me in this daily walk to excellence? Will you commit to seeking and submitting to God's will in every aspect of your everyday, ordinary life? We won't be able to use a measuring tape or statistical data to determine results. We'll be able to read the measuring rod in our hearts because we submitted our living to God and allowed him to direct our paths.

Please come walk with me in freedom from worry!

Father, help me to remember that you are in control of everything, and I'm not! Help me to submit to your will for my life and to stop worrying about things I cannot change.

Freedom from Captivity

Luci Swindoll

The LORD will guide you always; he will satisfy your needs in a sun-scorched land and will strengthen your frame.

—Isaiah 58:11a NIV

*I*n October 2002, Women of Faith watched a great adventure of love unfold before our eyes in an arena in Detroit. Everyone was completely stunned except one lovesick young man and our Women of Faith president, Mary Graham.

The young man, Mark Masterson, flew in from Turkey, where he was working, and hid out in our hotel. Just before the end of the conference on Saturday, Mary invited Dayna Curry onto the platform shortly before I spoke. The other speakers and I were surprised, but since we don't always know everything about the conference schedule in advance, it didn't seem too strange. Mary told some ridiculous story as Dayna stood dumbfounded by her side.

Suddenly, Mark ran down the aisle and bounded up on the platform, heading straight for Dayna. He knelt in front of her and, in the presence of twelve thousand women, asked her to marry him. Gratefully, after a moment of dead silence . . . she said yes. At that moment, everyone in the arena began cheering. We cried, whistled, applauded, stamped, and carried on like nobody in the history of the world had ever before gotten engaged. Everybody loves a lover, and we were seeing an exciting, romantic drama emerge before our eyes. Danya, who thought Mark was in Istanbul, had talked to him the night before on her cell phone, not knowing he was only two floors above her in the same hotel.

I believe part of the reason for our uncontrollable excitement was that only a year earlier, Dayna had been in a prison in Afghanistan. She was one of the two young women who had gone to that country as relief workers to help bring a better life and hope to some of the poorest and most oppressed people in the world. The other woman was her dear friend Heather Mercer. Both of them had spoken that morning in Detroit of what they experienced in their imprisonment and how their faith had been strengthened during those months, the scariest of their lives.

I'm sure you read about Dayna and Heather in the newspaper during those days. Within a few weeks of their arrival in Afghanistan, they were seized by the Taliban government and accused of talking with local people about Jesus and what he had done to change their lives. They were also indicted for showing a film about Jesus and how he held the hope for everyone in the world throughout all of history to be freed from spiritual bondage . . . even those who lived in Afghanistan.

In the midst of an international war against terrorism, Dayna and Heather were held hostage in four different prisons for 105 days. With the Taliban being a primary target of allied military forces, these wonderful young women didn't know if they would live or die from day to day. Christians all over the world began praying for their safe return to their families in America. In November 2001, our prayers were answered when they were released and allowed to come home. It's a story I encourage you to read for yourself in their wonderful book, *Prisoners of Hope: The Story of Our Captivity and Freedom in Afghanistan.*[1] In 2002, they were invited to be guest speakers for Women of Faith.

I heard Dayna and Heather share their story many times and was repeatedly spellbound by their words, manner, and humility. I got to know them personally, as did each of us on the team, and we were able to ask all the questions that came to mind and pray with them for their needs and those of their friends in Afghanistan. I saw and heard firsthand what it was like to take the voice of love, grace, and hope to those in bondage and hopelessness. Dayna and Heather were ambassadors not only for their local church but for all of us who value freedom and the right to life.

One of the greatest passages of Scripture that cries, "Freedom!" across the pages of history is from the hand of the prophet Isaiah. In chapter 61 of his book, he writes, "The Spirit of the Sovereign LORD is on me, because the LORD has anointed me to preach good news to the poor. He has sent me to bind up the brokenhearted, to proclaim freedom for the captives and release from darkness for the prisoners" (v. 1 NIV).

Dayna and Heather claimed this verse as their own. They had also read and believed Isaiah 58:10–11: "If you spend yourselves in behalf of the hungry and satisfy the needs of the oppressed, then your light will rise in the darkness . . . The LORD will guide you always; he will satisfy your needs in a sun-scorched land and will strengthen your frame" (NIV).

Afghanistan certainly qualified for being "a sun-scorched land," and the Afghan people were most definitely hungry and oppressed. So these two girls went on their mission trip in good faith, and God gave them a satisfaction they never dreamed of by means of his presence and miraculous deliverance. Interestingly, they were even freed by helicopter during the night so the light of their presence rose in darkness (literally), as Scripture promised.

Most of us won't experience such a dramatic opportunity to take the good news of freedom from captivity around the world, but we have been called and enabled to do that in our own neighborhood. Being in prison is not just bondage by a physical enemy, but it can also be something in our souls that holds us back from enjoying all that's available to us in Christ.

Jocelyn, for example, was a single mother with a six-year-old child. She met my friend Debbie a few weeks after her son had been killed in an automobile accident. Stricken with grief and full of sorrow, Jocelyn went to an apartment building, looking for a place to live. Debbie was moving in at the same time. After Jocelyn left, the landlord told Debbie Jocelyn's story. Being very compassionate and one who reaches out easily to strangers, Debbie called her and they became friends. Every day, Jocelyn simply went to work, came home, ate dinner, and went to bed. Her grief held her captive, and she was unable to overcome the emptiness in her life.

Debbie invited Jocelyn to go on walks with her. They walked, talked, cried together, and got to know each other. Jocelyn had been to church and read her Bible but enjoyed no assurance of salvation. She had no biblical understanding of God and was easily defeated. Debbie described Jocelyn as having "a shell of a life."

One day, Debbie planned to have lunch with Joyce (a friend who had also lost a child), and she invited Jocelyn to join them. As they visited, Joyce said, "Jocelyn, you need power to get through this period of your life . . . this loss. You need to know for sure that God is in your life, and you *can* know that for sure. You simply won't make it without God's power. I know that from my own experience." Debbie said they all prayed right there at the table, and Jocelyn invited Christ into her heart.

"When we left the restaurant, Jocelyn was different," Debbie said. "There was *life*. It was like somebody had pumped air into a flat tire."

Jocelyn began going to church and a Bible class. Several months later, Debbie gave her a study Bible, and on Christmas Eve Jocelyn showed her a verse she'd found: "You have turned for me my mourning into dancing; You have put off my sackcloth and clothed me with gladness" (Psalm 30:11 NKJV).

All of that was twenty years ago. The happy ending to the story is that Jocelyn is now married and has twin daughters who are seventeen. She loves the Lord and follows him wholeheartedly, day by day.

People all around us are brokenhearted. They're held captive by grief, regret, fear, poverty, legalism, and so much more. We who know the Savior hold the keys to their prison door. Scripture teaches that Christ has set us free, so we can *be* free. Those of us who know this from our own experience, like Joyce, can open that door for someone else, like Jocelyn.

When Joyce met Jocelyn, she had no idea she'd be the one God would use to bring a happy ending to that story of sadness.

There's also a happy ending for Dayna and Mark. They're married, living in West Africa, and expecting their first child. And Heather? She's spreading the gospel around the world. I get monthly letters telling how God is meeting needs and opening exciting opportunities for her to share the amazing message of freedom in Christ.

All these dear friends have given their lives to the cause of freedom. They take good news to the poor, bind up the brokenhearted, proclaim freedom to captives, and pray for prisoners to be released from darkness. It's phenomenal what God can do with hearts dedicated to him and hope that knows no boundaries.

Love and sacrifice speak loud enough to change the face of a nation and to set the spiritual captives free.

Thank you, Lord, for setting me free through Jesus Christ. Help me to open that door of freedom for someone else today.

Freedom from Stuff

Barbara Johnson

> Consider the lilies, how they grow: they neither toil
> nor spin; and yet I say to you, even Solomon in all
> his glory was not arrayed like one of these.
>
> —Luke 12:27 NKJV

Sometimes as I think about the last five years of my life, I see similarities to the pioneers who moved across America. When the pioneers moved from one home to the next, they packed their wagons with everything from pots and pans to pearls and pianos—the most practical and precious possessions they owned.

But something interesting often happened as the miles passed and the hardships began. Gradually, the pioneers' priorities changed as challenges confronted them on their journey. Beside a rain-swollen river, they might have discarded Grandmother's piano when it threatened to sink the wagon as they nervously forded the stream. At the foot of the mountains, many of them abandoned treasures or heirloom furniture.

In the middle of the desert, some even left behind the wagon and all its contents, emerging on the other side with nothing but their lives—and their faith in the future.

That's how Christians approach heaven: standing alone, empty handed, freed from all our "important" earthly priorities that litter the roadway behind us. It's the roadway that takes us to our Lord and Savior, who tells us, " Small is the gate and narrow the road that leads to life" (Matthew 7:14a NIV).

At times during the past year, when I've had to move from my comfortable home and live for a while in a convalescent center, I've empathized with those westward-moving pioneers who left behind their cherished possessions. It's been hard to turn loose of my things, even though nothing I own is all that valuable. In fact, some of my favorite "stuff" is downright silly. You may have heard of my Joy Room, the addition we built onto our mobile home to hold all the funny toys, jokes, plaques, gag gifts, and other smile makers I've collected since two of our sons were killed. The collection grew out of a shoebox I used to hold funny greeting cards, one-liners, and jokes friends sent to me or that I found wherever I traveled. When sadness threatened to overwhelm me, I would open my Joy Box and inevitably find something that made me smile or even laugh out loud.

Bill and I were never rich, but we were wealthy in having loving friends and family members and a room full of silly things that helped us push back the darkness of sorrow and stress. Surely those were the kinds of riches the writer of Ecclesiastes had in mind when he wrote, "When God gives any man wealth and possessions, and enables him to enjoy them, to accept his lot and be happy in his work—this is a gift of God" (5:19 NIV).

Leaving behind my Joy Room (and sometimes feeling like I was leaving behind all my *joy*, as well), I've moved into a room at the convalescent center for short or long visits as my health required. And each time, I've felt as though I'm moving through that narrow gate leading into God's waiting room, where it's just Jesus and me, getting back to basics. It's there that the words of Martin Luther's classic hymn "From Depths of Woe I Cry to Thee" seem so appropriate: "Before Thee none can boasting stand, but all must fear Thy strict demand and live alone by mercy."

For many years I have joked about ending up in the "Home for the Bewildered," and now here I am, bewildered by what's happening to me and able to go on through each new day, not because of anything I possess but only because of God's abiding mercy. In this small, bare room, I'm reminded repeatedly of the words of the apostle Paul, expressing his desire for the Corinthians—and Jesus' desire for all of us: "What I want is not your possessions but you" (2 Corinthians 12:14b NIV).

It's hard to give up our goods, but when we do, we find ourselves reaping an amazing benefit: the freedom to focus on what's *really* important. I'm reminded of a photo I love (it's reprinted in a couple of my books) that shows a rough plywood sign leaning against a pile of rubble, the remains of someone's home after devastating floods struck the Midwest in 1997. The sign, which said simply, "Store your treasures in heaven," was inspired by Matthew 6:19–20: "Do not store up for yourselves treasures on earth, where moth and rust destroy, and where thieves break in and steal. But store up for yourselves treasures in heaven, where moth and rust do not destroy, and where thieves do not break in and steal" (NIV).

Let's face it, our possessions can easily become our god. We want a nicer house, a fancier car, and a bigger diamond. And when we get those expensive and extravagant possessions, we lose our focus on what's important. Now we have to worry that our house will age, our car will get damaged, and the diamond will get lost. We focus on keeping those disasters from happening. As someone said, the more possessions we have, the more possessive we become.

One of my friends told me about a little boy who received a huge toy warship for Christmas. It was five feet long and loaded with realistic details, guns, and aircraft.

"Wow," my friend said to the boy's mother, "your son must have a great time playing with such a wonderful toy."

"Not really," his mother replied. "Mostly he just sits in his room and guards it from his younger siblings. He doesn't want any of them to play with it because he's sure they'll break it."

You have to wonder how much more fun the boy could have if he were freed from his possessive worries and could simply enjoy the gift he'd been given—or else leave it behind entirely and go play with his siblings and friends.

While Bill and I were traveling with Women of Faith, we took along several pieces of luggage because we had to take clothes for four days as well as things that were needed at the book table. One Sunday when Bill had unloaded the trunk of the car yet again after one of these trips, he announced that in the future we would travel only with carry-on luggage. "We don't need all this stuff," he said.

I agreed to give his suggestion a try, and on the next trip, we gleefully left the house with two carry-on roller bags, a tote bag, and my purse. After we checked into the hotel, instead of having to wait for the bellman to bring up our luggage, we wheeled our bags right up to our room and settled in immediately. "Oh, I feel so free!" I told Bill. "This is great."

We felt unencumbered, almost giddy. A load had been taken off of us (literally!) because we'd been freed from all that unnecessary baggage. What joy! We had learned to travel light.

All went well until the return flight home. As Bill's carry-on bag went through security, the screener pulled it off the line. He quickly found what he'd spotted on the X-ray. "You can't take this on the plane," he said.

"What do you mean? I *brought* it on the plane when we flew out here," Bill argued, frustrated that we were being delayed.

"Well, they should have caught it. You can't travel with anything that can be used as a weapon," the agent replied.

Bill was miffed, but he knew he didn't have a choice. The screener kept the forbidden item, a box cutter Bill used to open our boxes of books. In the past it had been in our checked luggage, so it hadn't caused a problem. But that sharp-eyed screener had caught it when Bill's carry-on bag was X-rayed.

That did it. "No more carry-on bags for us," Bill said. He fumed about the incident for months. (Bill was very frugal, so having to give up *anything* involuntarily was a problem for him.) But his attitude changed on 9/11, when the planes that were used in the attack on America were hijacked by heartless men wielding—you guessed it—box cutters.

Still, I look back at that incident as a precursor to the time when cancer would force me to "travel light" for the rest of my days.

It's been an amazing experience to find, in my losses, an enlightening freedom. Illness can be a burden, yes. But it can also free us to focus on what's really important. And that one thing is Jesus, waiting for us on the other side of the narrow gate, just past the piles of rubble we once considered treasures.

Jesus, nothing matters to me now but you. Please
keep my feet on the narrow road, and don't let
anything come between us!

Freedom from Condemnation

Marilyn Meberg

Yet now God in his gracious kindness declares us
not guilty. He has done this through Christ Jesus,
who has freed us by taking away our sins.

—Romans 3:24 NLT

*W*ith all the earnestness of an imprisoned soul, five-year-old Jeff said to me one night at bedtime, "Mama, I need a lot more freedom. I need the freedom to play as long as I want to. And I don't like having to go to bed so early either. Mama, this is not working for me."

My response was, "You know, baby, I often think the same thing. I wish I, too, had more freedom to do what I want."

With a disappointed sigh, Jeff turned away from me, saying simply, "Good night, Mama."

Deep down, we all desire more freedom. Jesus appealed to our elemental quest for freedom when he said, "Then you will know the truth, and the truth will set you free" (John 8:32 NIV). But what "truth" will enable us to experience the freedom we so desperately desire? Jesus made that clear when he declared, "I am the way and *the truth* and the life" (John 14:6 NIV; emphasis added). Jesus' promise of freedom comes from knowing truth and from himself, because he is that truth.

So what does that mean to us? Plain and simple, it means we have no freedom apart from Jesus Christ.

To be without freedom is to be enslaved. As Jesus said, "I assure you that everyone who sins is a slave of sin" (John 8:34 NLT). But the plan of a loving God was to prevent the enslavement of his creation. Romans 8:3 says, "God put into effect a different plan to save us. He sent his own Son in a human body like ours, except that ours are sinful. God destroyed sin's control over us by giving his Son as a sacrifice for our sins" (NLT). The result of Jesus' sacrifice is this: "So now there is no condemnation for those who belong to Christ Jesus. For the power of the life-giving Spirit has freed you through Christ Jesus from the power of sin that leads to death" (Romans 8:1–2 NLT).

Those incredible truths are the emancipation proclamations for all believers. We are free—free because of Jesus.

But let me ask you this. Do you feel free? If you do feel free, you believe that you truly are without condemnation. But I've lived on the earth long enough to know that a great majority of us find it too big a stretch to believe we stand before God each day without condemnation. It sounds great, but for many of us it's a truth we can't grasp; it is not realistic.

I received a letter from a woman who was anguishing

over her inability to give up her sin. She knew what she was doing was sin, but she couldn't seem to stop herself. She had been divorced five years from a man who demeaned her, criticized her, and was unfaithful to her. When he left, she felt abandoned and unworthy. A year after the divorce, she met a man who thought she was beautiful, intelligent, and fun. He said all the things her parched soul longed to hear. The only problem: he was married. Knowing full well what she should do, she gave into what she shouldn't do.

The affair was still in full swing when she wrote to me. Her question was, does God still love her when she is choosing to live in sin? Is she living without condemnation? Does Romans 8:1 apply to her? Does God see us without condemnation as long as we live according to his standards, or does he actually love us and see us without condemnation even when we're sinning up a storm and ignoring his standards?

According to the human system we are used to, if we blow it, ignore the rules, and do what we feel like, we will be fired, rejected, or at least strongly reprimanded. That's the system. But God does not use our system; that's why many of us miss it. Remember, Scripture tells us, "God put into effect a different plan to save us" (Romans 8:3 NLT).

The old plan makes sense to us because it was a rule-keeping system. That system was initiated by God when he gave the Ten Commandments to Moses on the Israelites' way to the Promised Land.

When Moses began teaching his people God's laws and the consequences of breaking those laws, at least the people knew what God expected of them. All they had to do was follow the rules. The problem? They kept breaking the rules; they were too hard to follow. A person might be able to follow the rule about not killing her neighbor, for example, but how would she keep from coveting her neighbor's tent, husband, sandals, or robe? As soon as the rules extended from outer behavior to the inner life, the challenges became enormously difficult for rule keeping.

The people realized they were unable to keep God's laws as stated in the Ten Commandments. If they could not keep his laws, they could not please him; they could not be acceptable to him. Why could they not keep the laws? They had a sin-prone nature. Pleasing God and being acceptable to him looked hopeless.

The apostle Paul wrote the book of Romans to believers who needed to understand the difference between the God's "different plan" and the old Ten Commandments plan. Paul says, "The law of Moses could not save us, because of our sinful nature" (Romans 8:3 NLT). Then he explains, "But now we have been released from the law, for we died with Christ, and we are no longer captive to its power. Now we can really serve God, not in the old way by obeying the letter of the law, but in the new way, by the Spirit" (Romans 7:6 NLT).

In yet another clarification of God's intent with the law, Paul writes, "So just as sin ruled over all people and brought them to death, now God's wonderful kindness rules instead, giving us right standing with God and resulting in eternal life through Jesus Christ our Lord" (Romans 5:21 NLT). We have been set free from the law requiring perfect behavior.

Most of us are aware of the continuing presence of our sin nature, even though Jesus released us from the condemnation of that nature. So what does this freedom from our sin nature mean for us? And what about the woman caught in an affair her heart and body can't seem to walk away from? As we asked earlier, is she truly without condemnation as she stands before God? Are we?

The answer is yes. We truly stand before God and are not condemned. To be condemned is to be pronounced guilty. The death of Jesus, who took to the cross this woman's sin of infidelity as well as our sin, provides forgiveness and freedom from condemnation. Mind boggling, isn't it? It goes against our system of paying for what you do.

The sobering reality for this woman, as for all of us, is we will indeed pay consequences for sin. But the consequences are the result of poor choices, poor judgment, and selfish inclinations—all of which originate from a choice to sin.

We often confuse human consequences with divine judgment. Scripture makes it clear that if we are in Christ, we are not condemned; therefore, we are not judged for our sins. I believe, however, God uses and even orchestrates consequences as a way of instructing us in the wisdom of not yielding to our sin nature in the future. God is in all things, and in all things his intent is to draw us closer to himself. His intent is that we drink more deeply from his well of love, forgiveness, and grace. His intent is also that we rest in the security of his forgiveness, which sets us free from condemnation.

To help me remember and put into practice the freedom I have in Christ, I have memorized the following freedom-producing words. Perhaps you, too, will find these words freeing.

For all have sinned; all fall short of God's glorious standard. Yet now God in his gracious kindness declares us not guilty. He has done this through Christ Jesus, who has freed us by taking away our sins. For God sent Jesus to take the punishment for our sins and to satisfy God's anger against us. We are made right with God when we believe that Jesus shed his blood, sacrificing his life for us. God was being entirely fair and just when he did not punish those who sinned in former times. And he is entirely fair and just in this present time when he declares sinners to be right in his sight because they believe in Jesus. (Romans 3:23–26 NLT)

God, thank you for forgiving my sins and setting me from condemnation. Help me today to drink more deeply from your well of love, forgiveness, and grace.

Freedom from Fear

Mary Graham

Do not be afraid. I bring you good news of great
joy that will be for all the people.

—Luke 2:10 NIV

*M*y parents died, six weeks apart, in the spring of 1982. Though their deaths weren't sudden, the impact of losing them so close together was emotionally overwhelming. Because I'd been part of the caretaking team with my other siblings, I'd had what I would have thought was time to prepare for the loss. Nothing, however, could have prepared me for what happened in my life after they died.

In those days, a huge part of my work with Campus Crusade for Christ required air travel, as it had for many years. Traveling not just in the States but also around the world was routine for me. I flew as a part of my ongoing work responsibility, and I often found myself on assignments that necessitated additional travel.

I took my first airplane trip as a young teenager flying alone from Tulsa to Los Angeles. From that first flight, I felt right at home on an airplane; it seemed like a good way to get from one place to another. Flying was a means to an end for me—nothing more, nothing less.

Until my parents died. My mother's death was in late March, and my dad's death less than two months later. Losing them had taken a toll on our whole family. I decided to take a month-long sabbatical from my work. That was something I'd been encouraged to do for a few years but never seemed to find the right time. Overwhelmed by grief and fatigue, this seemed like the perfect opportunity.

When I went back to work, my first assignment was in Colorado. I don't remember anything unusual about the flight from LA to Denver, but when I was flying home a few days later, I was seated in an aisle seat toward the front, buckled in with my newspaper in my lap as the pilot raced down the runway. As we lifted off into the clear blue sky, out of the blue, I felt a rush of fear about the plane. That had never happened to me before.

In the six months immediately following that incident, every time I was on a plane, I felt afraid. In time, my fear became absolute terror to the point of wondering how I could manage emotionally on a plane. So I started looking for a way out of air travel or at least tried to find a way for someone I knew to be with me on every flight.

By the late fall of that year, I was a mess. I wasn't talking with anybody about my fear, but it was in complete control of my life. I dreaded every trip, and each one was a challenge I tried to avoid. I talked my way out of meetings and turned down invitations to speak. Finally, my friends caught on and started the conversations that exposed my angst.

Never in my life have I suffered from anything so controlling as the fear of flying. I thought about it all the time when I flew, when I was not on a plane, and even when I didn't have a trip scheduled. I would never have imagined or believed how completely in fear's grip I was.

During those days, my fear of flying controlled me. After years and years of trusting God with my schedule, my life, and my ministry, I was taking matters into my own hands. It didn't matter who wanted me to go where or why, my initial response was always no.

I thought for weeks about what it meant to trust God and what it meant to be obedient. I was concerned that my fear would grow so that I'd be not only afraid to fly but afraid to leave the house at all.

Then Christmas came. I was scheduled to be with my sister and her family in Anchorage, Alaska, a pilgrimage I had made every year they'd been stationed there with my brother-in-law's work. One of my nieces has Down syndrome, and I knew she would not understand if I didn't make the trip. It was the only thing that could motivate me to go. I begged a friend to go with me, which she graciously agreed to do. Nonetheless, the long flight was a nightmare. I kept changing my seat and my position in it. I held on and then let go. I was terrified.

When we arrived, I felt only panic, knowing the trip back was a short week away. The next day, I read the Christmas story and began to see how fear was a common thread throughout the biblical account. In Luke 1, Zechariah was afraid when the angel announced to him the birth of Christ. Also in Luke, Mary's first response was to be afraid. In the Gospel of Matthew, we are told that Joseph was afraid. And, in the second chapter of Luke, we learn that the shepherds were not only afraid, but they were *sore* afraid. (That made sense to me. I was so afraid I did feel sore!) In every case, the angel of the Lord was reassuring, always using the same phrase with frightened people: "Fear not."

The Christmas story is the greatest story ever told—there's never been better news in all of history than the news that God the Father sent Jesus to redeem the world of sin. News has never been that great, yet people were afraid. Afraid of what? The unknown, their own feelings, their own lack of understanding, their own helplessness, their own inability to know the plan, understand it, or control it.

Suddenly this all made a little more sense to me than it had before. Getting on that plane on December 26 wasn't as frightening as it had been just a week earlier. I was flying to the Midwest to speak to university students at a conference. In the course of my remarks, I mentioned what I was learning about fear and admitted for the first time how afraid I'd been and how much I had suffered because of my fear of flying.

When I finished my message, a woman came up to me and said, "I'm here because I know some of the students. I'm a therapist, and I might be able to help you with your fear." We sat for a while, and she asked me a lot of questions about my experiences in the past year. Without really knowing why, I mentioned the death of my folks. She probed a good bit and finally rested there. She explained how losing them might have triggered some fear in me that seemed irrational and unrelated but wasn't. I was surprised, but the more she talked, the more what she said made sense to me.

By the end of our conversation, I gained tremendous insight about how inadvertently I made flying the object of my consternation about my parents' deaths. Within hours, my dismay was no longer paralyzing. Something about understanding the root of my fear dissipated its power. I sensed the Lord's voice when she said to me in so many words, "Fear not."

I don't have a professional understanding of these things, and I have never tried to take my experience and make it relevant nor applicable to anyone else's. But this I know: I was desperately caught in a cycle of fear and hopelessness, and my life felt on hold as a result. Between God's Word and the words of a professional counselor, I started making my way back to freedom, and it was amazing.

Little did I know then that now I'd be flying several times a week. Between the Women of Faith conferences on the week-ends and meetings during the week, I'm often on as many as five flights a week. Walking onto a plane is no different for me than walking into a room. I don't like the inconvenience flying has become, but I can honestly say it doesn't scare me.

I know many people who are afraid to fly, and interestingly, I often meet them on planes. I feel empathic when they tell me of their fear and very sympathetic with their need. I'm aware that my simple story won't change how they feel. What happened to me is hardly universal.

However, one thing I know is that for me the fear was tied to something not at all connected to airplanes. And I know God gave me the insight and the help I needed to become free from that fear. Whatever is going on in my life, and however I happen to be processing it at any given time, I can be sure that my real freedom comes not from figuring out what troubles me or why. Real freedom comes from knowing the God of the universe is a great and mighty God, One who is in complete control and who can be completely trusted. As the angel said to the shepherds, "Do not be afraid. I bring you good news of great joy that will be for *all* the people" (Luke 2:10 NIV; emphasis added).

We are *all* free because of this great joy. Free even from fear.

God, no matter what comes into my life today, help
me obey what you say: "Fear not!"

Freedom from Busyness

Thelma Wells

Come unto Me, all you who labor and are heavy
laden, and I will give you rest.

—Matthew 11:28 NKJV

*E*very person needs to take a break from the busyness
of life to do something relaxing and refreshing during
the year. Personally, I like taking retreats.

April 2005 was a great and rewarding month for me. I
spent most of my time attending retreats that were places of
relaxation, relief, renewal, restoration, and rejuvenation.

The first retreat brought twelve people to our home, which
we call the "Haven on the Lake." I had not seen some of these
ladies for three years because of my speaking schedule. My
Sunday school class, the Truth Seekers, traveled to my home
for a reunion of all three Sunday school teachers: Debra, who
moved away; Nona, our current teacher; and Thelma (that's
me), the former teacher. We hugged and hugged, laughed

until our sides hurt, cried buckets of tears, ate until we were rolling instead of walking, watched speakers on DVD, and listened to some of the most beautiful praise music in the world. But the highlight of the weekend was the testimonies of the ladies.

One lady, who is going through cancer treatment, drove from Houston to the retreat in Dallas. She was assured that God would do something special in her. He did. She was encouraged and strengthened with the hope that she could go through this ordeal knowing Jesus is with her every step of the way.

Another lady had strayed away from church because she had experienced so many losses in her life. Even though she loves God, she didn't want to be around church people. At the retreat, her faith in people was restored and she rededicated her life to Christ and renewed her commitment to her local church.

Another retreat I participated in was in the hill country of Texas near San Antonio. We were out in the woods on a campsite with people of several nationalities and denominations. That group of forty women was a virtual melting pot. Everyone there reported realizing the presence, peace, and power of God, and one lady accepted Christ. And yes, we bunked together, laughed together, played games, enjoyed a barn fire, got several sugar rushes from the sweets, prayed together, sang together, and traveled in a caravan together.

Then I went to another retreat, where I spent time with thirty ladies I didn't know, along with my doctor and her sister-in-law, in Horseshoe, Texas. Even though it rained the entire weekend, it was so pretty and green with all the luxurious amenities of a five-star resort. We enjoyed casual clothes, warm conversations, delicious food, active learning, and a birthday party, and ministry anointing was the order of the weekend. It was the perfect setting for Jesus to come in and heal. He did!

Sometimes we become tired and burned out; we get so overburdened with the chores and routines of the day that we get irritable and cranky. Sometimes we even take our emotions out on other people. We give and give, take on other people's responsibilities, push ourselves past our limits, and berate ourselves if we don't do for others. I don't know whether you take some time for yourself during the day or not. But if you don't, you need to.

I know what you're thinking: *I don't have time to do all the things I need to do, let alone take time for me. Even if I try to take time for me somebody will interrupt me or need something.*

I used to feel that same way. There were not enough hours in the day for all I had to do, I thought. I was working a full-time job, carpooling, doing the laundry, cooking, going to meetings and church, and all the other things that go along with being a wife, mother, and community leader. I remember when my oldest child turned sixteen. I forced her to get her driver's license so I would have one less child to transport to extracurricular activities. That was triumphant and traumatic, but we made it.

But look at God. He created the world in six days and then *rested* on the seventh. If God rested, we need to follow his lead.

Do you remember when Jesus left the masses of people to go rest? The crowd followed him, but he still had a chance to regroup. When he met the Samaritan woman at Jacob's well, he was resting and refreshing himself. We *need* to take time to rest. Don't wait until you are forced to rest by breaking a limb or getting sick or losing your job. Get rejuvenated while things are going well.

Take a much-needed vacation before the doctor prescribes one for you. Go to a quiet place for a day or so. Take a drive in the country just for the fun of it. Relax in the bathtub for an hour without allowing anyone to disturb you. Go bike riding, roller-skating, swimming, go-cart driving, or something that's relaxing to you. Just sit and be bored for an hour. Read a book, play the piano, play a board game, listen to music, watch television, listen to the radio, go to a movie, eat by yourself, stay at home and don't put on makeup or get dressed for the day, or have a mother-daughter day, a girlfriend day, or a just-for-me day. Do something to break the monotony of your life.

After I had attended all these retreats, I guess God knew I needed some added rest. I like to think that he "ar-*rest*-ed" me for his cause. I had four months of much-needed rest—

although I'd rather not have gotten it the way I did. I was bedridden from two surgeries. When you are on your back in bed, God has your attention. What else can you do? So my rest was more than a source of physical healing; it was a major force of spiritual awakening. I learned patience because I could not do anything for myself. I learned humility because it is very humbling to have people do things for you that you used to do for yourself. The rest I got helped change my perspective on work.

God has provided 168 hours every week to do everything we need to do. God knew that we could not go like the Energizer bunny day in and day out. Our batteries will run out eventually. That's why sleep time is a part of our rest and relaxation time. It has been said that if you don't get eight to ten hours of sleep per twenty-four-hour period, you are not getting ample rest. When we don't rest, our bodies and minds break down.

Personally, I've gotten enough rejuvenation to last me a long time. But you know how it is when you receive all that power; you need rebooting soon. That's why Women of Faith is so good for me. For nearly thirty weeks a year, I'm rebooted by the presence and power of God at the largest retreat I've ever attended, with more than ten thousand women singing, praying, laughing, and crying together. What a joy! What an awesome opportunity to let it all hang out with my girlfriends from all walks of life!

Many women's ministry groups attend the Women of Faith conference as their women's retreat. Family members from all over the country meet at the conference for a girls' family reunion. High school and college friends, sorority sisters, and other organizations journey to the conference for fun, frolic, and faith. Those who've come before know they will find a heartfelt welcome, laughter, comfort, safety, encouragement, inspiration, and enrichment within the walls of the arena.

I urge you to plan your own retreat. Take time to experience freedom from the business of your life, and get away with two or three other ladies. Study the Word, tell your story, cry, pray, sing, and watch God give you his presence, his peace, and his power!

—

Lord, I commit to you today that I will take a break from the busyness of my life to do something relaxing and refreshing.

Freedom from Anger

Sheila Walsh

> But the Spirit produces the fruit of love, joy, peace, patience, kindness, goodness, faithfulness, gentleness, self-control. There is no law that says these things are wrong. Those who belong to Christ Jesus have crucified their own sinful selves. They have given up their old selfish feelings and the evil things they wanted to do.
>
> —Galatians 5:22–24 NCV

I remember the first time I stepped inside an airplane and strapped my body into what would become a flying seat. I was very excited. I was nineteen years old and a student at seminary in London, England. My budget would never have extended to an airplane ticket, but I had been invited to sing at an evangelistic crusade in Edinburgh, Scotland, and a plane ticket was included in the invitation.

I watched as the flight attendant demonstrated how to fasten the seatbelt and showed us where the life vests were located. I was slightly alarmed at the suggestion that we could use our seat bottoms as floating devices. I had no desire to float; I wanted to fly. Then came the instruction for the oxygen masks. By this point, I was wondering if we were now at war and I had missed the news. As the plane began to gather speed for takeoff, I started to laugh. I have no idea why other than it seemed a better response than grabbing the knee of the man I was sitting beside.

Now I fly thousands of miles a year. I have probably accumulated enough frequent-flyer miles for a free DC10, but I have nowhere to park it. All this to say that I consider flying as routine as brushing my teeth. However, every now and then something happens to shake me out of my business-as-usual mentality.

The trip started out as any other. I always allow two hours to get from my home in North Dallas to the airport. Without traffic accidents, I can make it in about thirty minutes—but in this part of Texas we specialize in traffic accidents, as was the case on this particular Thursday. By the time I got to the check-in desk, I still had an hour before my flight, so I wasn't concerned. In front of me in line were a mom and her daughter, who must have been three or four years old. She was a very cute little girl with big blue eyes and a blonde ponytail. She was holding a doll whose dress had gotten wet when she spilled some water on it. The mom was reassuring her that the doll would be fine, but the little girl did not seem convinced. The mom took the doll and placed it on top of her luggage cart to dry.

Soon it was their turn to check in. I turned my attention to my purse and was looking for my driver's license when I heard the first outburst.

"You've got to be kidding me!" the mother yelled so loudly that airline employees in several booths stopped what they were doing and turned to see what had happened.

The girl behind the counter was trying to explain to this irate woman that it is federal aviation policy that passengers must check in a certain amount of time before a flight or their bags will not be accepted. As it was only twenty minutes before their flight, the machine would not issue tags.

"There is nothing I can do, ma'am," she said. "I will be happy to book you on the next flight."

"That is completely unacceptable!" she cried, pushing her luggage to one side so violently that everything fell off the cart. The little girl bent down and picked up her doll. By this point the woman was now on her cell phone with her husband, presumably, and was screaming at him.

"This is your fault! You can't do anything right!"

I looked down at the little girl as she pulled the doll tight against her chest as if to protect her from the storm of words. My heart ached for this little one who had learned to comfort herself by comforting one who seemed weaker and more vulnerable. I was sure this was not the first verbal blizzard she had lived through.

Words have the ability to shine like diamonds or pierce like daggers. Words can make a child feel that they can fly or teach them to never even look up. As I passed through security that day, I prayed for the little girl, and I prayed for the mom too. She was out of control, and that is a terrible way to live. She had cursed at the girl behind the ticket counter and her husband in a voice loud enough to make passers-by stop and stare. Through it all, her child kept her gaze fixed on the top of her doll's head.

As someone who has struggled with anger, I felt empathy for this woman. I have never raised my voice like that to my son Christian, but I have to Barry. Being out of control is a frightening experience. Words shoot out like tiny hand-crafted missiles designed to hit the target in question. Although it has only happened two or three times, I have seen the aftermath of that kind of onslaught, and it has filled me with deep regret. So much so that after the second time I exploded at Barry in anger, I made an appointment to see a Christian counselor.

I gave him a brief description of what had taken place and asked for his input.

"Do you want the long answer or the short answer?" he asked.

"As you charge by the hour, I'll go with the short one," I replied.

"Then stop it," he said.

"I beg your pardon . . . that's it? Just 'stop it'?" I asked. "I think I'd better go with the long one."

"Sheila, do you believe that as a Christian you are filled with the Holy Spirit?" he asked.

"Yes, of course," I replied.

"What do you understand to be the purpose of the Holy Spirit in your life?"

"To teach me to love God, to worship, to become like Jesus," I answered.

"When you lose control and raise your voice at Barry, where is the Holy Spirit then?" he questioned.

"Well, he probably went off to check on Billy Graham," I replied flippantly. "Sorry. I mean, I know that my words and my heart grieve him."

"When you find yourself in a place like this again and you feel anger beginning to rise, then stop. Stop and ask the Holy Spirit to help you. Get down on your knees and throw yourself at the throne of mercy," he said with great compassion.

His advice that day sounded too simple. I wanted to respond, "Well, easy for you to say!" but I knew that he had given me the simple gift of the truth. In Galatians 5:22–23, the apostle Paul writes that "the fruit of the Spirit is love, joy, peace, patience, kindness, goodness, faithfulness, gentleness and self-control" (NIV). Fruit is produced; it doesn't just appear. It is a growth process as the fruit cooperates with the tree. There is much that happens beneath the surface of the branches before any fruit is seen at all. I saw clearly that day that if I want to be a godly woman, I have to cooperate with the Holy Spirit and not ignore those gentle urgings to surrender my broken humanity.

I would love to tell you that I have never raised my voice again, but that would not be true. What is true is that raising my voice to Barry is now very, very rare. I have discovered that the spiritual discipline of lining my will up with the will of God, whether I feel like it or not, is life-changing. When I want to cry out, "I can't help it!" I hear his gentle voice reply: *I can.*

I don't know what issue you might be struggling with today, but I know you are not alone. The Holy Spirit is a Master Gardener who delights in working with scrawny, out-of-control bushes if they will yield to his gentle pruning.

Father God, I want to be more like Jesus. I ask you to help me today to surrender my sinful nature to your careful pruning so that I can be free to love you. Teach me to love those whose lives my life will touch today.

Freedom from Financial Worry

Nicole Johnson

> If you sinful people know how to give good gifts to
> your children, how much more will your heavenly
> Father give good gifts to those who ask him.
>
> —Matthew 7:11 NLT

"An actress? You want to be an actress?" Actually, my
family probably knew this long before I did. As a
very dramatic little girl, I cared more about emotions than
emoting. So I don't think anyone in my family was surprised
to hear my ambition. Just worried.

But to their credit, they kept their worries and their fears
to themselves. I know they had worries and fears, because
we've discussed them since, but they believed very much
that God would lead me, as did I. And none of us were wrong.

There is great freedom in trusting God with your life. We
are set free to pursue our greatest dreams and deepest calling. When we trust God with our lives, we are given, by God
of course, the chance to utilize and maximize our gifts in

this world—and that can set us free from the worry that so easily besets us. Because God has called us and because he has gifted us, he will help us. It's the greatest news ever—he is there, in some ways like a safety net under the high wire, ready to catch us if we fall.

But we don't always see this on our own, and sometimes people are like "glasses from God" to help us see this more clearly. Such was the case with my stepfather, David.

David and I are very close, and by his own admission he never set out to be my father. ("You have a good father already," he would say, and it's true.) So David became a friend and an incredible support and strength in my life.

He and my mother were leaving to go overseas to visit his daughter. They had planned to be gone for two months or so and would not be accessible while they were away on their trip. Hard to believe, even as I write this, but that's how it was in the "olden days" before the Internet and cell phones.

Several weeks earlier, I had expressed some concern to them of my having "more month than money." I wasn't in financial trouble at all; I just had a financial question mark on this particular season. I was still fresh in my career and couldn't always count on consistent cash flow. At times, I would worry out loud. I didn't need money, I assured them, just a good reminder of who is in control of my finances.

Upon their departure, David handed me two checks. He said that he wanted to leave them for me in case I needed money while they were gone. I was very touched, but I did my best to reassure them that I would be fine and that they didn't need to leave me any money. I was grateful, though I couldn't know at the time how much it would free me.

It was clear Mom and Dad believed in me—but that they would leave me money, just in case, was a comfort and a relief. I could go on about my business without being saddled by my concern that something would happen and I would get stuck in a financial bind. It was very freeing.

And while that gesture was special and generous and very significant in its own right, what happened after they were gone will stay with me for the rest of my life. It's as clear a picture of love and freedom as any I've ever gotten.

The financial question mark never materialized, and everything worked out fine. I didn't need any money, and the short-term anxiety subsided. But through the process I often thought of the checks and what it meant to me to have that kind of support to back me up. Just having the checks on my desk reminded me daily of the love and care of my parents.

The day it became clear that I wouldn't need the money, I wondered if I should void the checks or tear them up to let my folks know that I hadn't used them. That's when it dawned on me that David had written me *two blank checks* out of his own bank account. I just sat there looking at the pieces of paper in front of me on my desk.

My folks were still out of the country, but my heart just flew to them. I wanted to call, I wanted to dance, I wanted to jump around like a crazy woman—but in a few moments I had my head in my hands. David left me everything he had, just in case I needed it. A few words from the old hymn "How Great Thou Art" come to mind: "I scarce can take it in."

I'm sure the parallel between David and our heavenly Father is not lost on you. God is there for us in bigger ways than we could ever think to even ask. Not only does he anticipate our needs, but he provides for them generously beyond what we would have imagined.

When God calls us, he will fan the flame of our passion and even fund the efforts on his behalf. How he does it is different for everyone, but the fact that he does it is not. He has written you a blank check to help you pursue the calling that he has placed upon your life. His resources do not run out. His bank account is not limited. He trusts you to call on him as you need him—time and again. His great satisfaction is seeing you using your gifts to make a difference in this world.

I have kept both checks. They are tucked securely in a box of my most special cards and remembrances, and I will treasure them for the rest of my life. And when I feel uncertain about my future or wonder if I have what it takes to keep going, financially and otherwise, I need only to look at those checks for a tangible reminder of God's love and care. We can be set free from worry because of his incredible, personal, daily provision for our needs.

Scripture might say it this way: "If David, being an earthly father, knows how to give gifts like that to you, how much more does your heavenly Father know about how to supply all of your needs?" (see Matthew 7:11).

We can experience freedom when we trust that God offers us a limitless supply of love and care with our names on it.

———

Father, show me how to trust you for provision. Remind me often, as I forget, that you are in control of all things, my bank account included. Set me free from worry when I become afraid that you aren't going to be there. Let me dance in the abundance that you have promised and delivered in more ways than I can count.

Freedom from Perfectionism

Patsy Clairmont

Therefore we do not lose heart. Even though our outward man
is perishing, yet the inward man is being renewed day by day.
For our light affliction, which is but for a moment, is working
for us a far more exceeding and eternal weight of glory.

—2 Corinthians 4:16–17 NKJV

I just came in from taking a walk. (Every once in a while,
I get a burst of incentive and decide to become aerobic—well, my condensed version of aerobic.) As I walked, I
couldn't help but delight in the day. It was 65 degrees and
sunny, the birds were celebrating with chipper songs, butterflies seemed giddy as they flitted over shrubs and flowers, the
daffodils touted their yellow petals like children in Easter
outfits, and the pansies crowded together and hung over the
planters, giggling as I huffed and puffed by.

Then suddenly I was stopped in my tracks when I spotted
on the sidewalk in front of me a petrified frog—deader than
a doornail, on its back, and appearing freeze-dried. May I
just say . . . yuck! The frog reminded me of Edvard Munch's

painting *The Scream*. The crusty critter seemed frozen in terror, mouth open, little legs hardened into what looked like escape mode.

I had really gotten into the sights and fresh smells of this spring day when this frog "hopped" into view. Why is it that in the midst of so much good a fossilized reptile must appear? Hmm, I guess that's sort of a picture of life on this earth. Even with fastidious planning and the finest of intentions, things sometimes croak up.

For instance, have you ever attended a wedding where a mishap didn't occur? In the midst of lace, netting, white roses, and lit candles, all too often someone passes out, throws up, says the wrong name, sings off key, or forgets their cue.

At my son's wedding, three of the five men in the wedding party struggled throughout the entire service to stay conscious—one had locked his knees (which caused him to turn green and sway like a wind-blown palm tree), one was sweating bullets from sheer fear and couldn't seem to remember to breathe, and one was weakened by food poisoning and had to be steadied by the bride.

Or what about having company over for dinner? The house is sparkling from all your efforts, the table setting looks like it's right out of *House Beautiful*, and the aroma of food is scrumptious. Then you go to check on the rolls and find Fido on a chair wolfing down your glorious pineapple-studded ham. As you scream, he quickly takes one more mouthful and scampers for cover, flinging bits of your dinner in his path.

Yep, into everyone's life a petrified frog must hop.

We can't imagine at the moment that these types of blunders will become great stories and cherished memories. We're often too mortified by our immediate need to stage perfection to see the humanity and humor in it. For often, in a quirky way, these faux pas take the important event and kick it up a notch with the vitality that comes with the unexpected.

I have to remind myself that we live in a fallen world and that nothing is going to be perfect here. Everything is slightly askew. Perhaps you've heard a salesperson try to fluff up a tainted item with a line like, "Oh, that little flaw—well, actually it adds character to the piece. It makes it more valuable."

I bought a new bed last year. When it was delivered, I noticed that it had several "character spots" in the form of nicks in the wood. I pointed them out to the deliverymen, and one of the chaps pulled out a touch-up pen from his pocket and colored in the blemishes. Then he looked at me and smiled, as if to say, "All better." He, of course, didn't change the fact that the nicks were still there; he just made the "character" less noticeable and more tolerable (sort of like when I apply makeup).

When I decided to relax about the less-than-perfect bed, I found out I slept just as well despite the nicks.

Perhaps therein lies our freedom as we make peace with

the fact our world is nicked, imperfect, and faulty, and we are surrounded by defective people . . . including us.

Ribbet.

When we become more comfortable with the imperfections in life, not only are we not so easily thrown by defects as they hop into view, but we discover more about ourselves.

I read about an artist who, following a brush with death, changed her approach to her work. Instead of trying so hard to please other frogs . . . ahem, I mean people, and rather than following the lead of other artists and trying to jump on their lily pads, she began to go deeper within herself to find her own unique expression. The initial result of her new-found freedom is that her art was just featured in a ten-page spread in an international magazine.

The unexpected frog (brush with death) in the road of this artist's life helped to free her of insecurities that were holding her back artistically.

My friend Carol has always been artistic. In fact, I can remember when we were children how I admired her artsy flair. As we grew older, I decided she should do more with this gift. Don't you love it when someone else thinks they know what you should do? Of course it didn't make a bit of difference what my plans were for Carol's life because God didn't ask me to be in charge of her. Shoot! It wasn't until years later that Carol decided she wanted to grow in her gift and signed up take an art class in her neighborhood.

Get this: the first night of the first class, when the owner of the art store saw her work, he hired Carol on the spot to train his instructors. Yes, his *instructors*.

I love that story, not because I was right (well, maybe a little), but because my shy friend found a liberating path that would help her to step around that croaking frog of timidity.

Recently, my friend Jennifer sent me a powerful quote that rings with truth from Hawthorne's *The House of Seven Gables*: "She had been enriched by poverty, developed by sorrow, elevated by the strong and solitary affection of her life and thus endowed with heroism which never could have characterized her in what are called happier circumstances."

The line that especially caught my eye was "developed by sorrow."

Lucy Maud Montgomery from Prince Edward Island and author of the Anne of Green Gables book series was deeply acquainted with sorrows even as a child. If sorrows were a frog, Lucy had a plaque.

When Lucy was twenty-one months old, her mother died of tuberculosis. Her father left Lucy with her mother's parents, and then he left the island. Now without either of her parents, she found herself living in a colorless, solemn home of grieving grandparents.

No wonder Lucy wrote of an orphan girl searching for a place to belong—but what is surprising is that the story is so upbeat and full of fun. Many feel Lucy survived because of her passion for nature and by escaping into the world of the delightful characters she created.

Lucy's losses didn't end in her childhood, for it seems the longer any of us lives, the more losses we all experience. When Lucy's grandfather died, she moved in with her grandmother to keep her from losing her home. Her grandmother lived for thirteen more years. Then Lucy married a pastor who suffered from deep melancholy. She bore him three sons, one of whom died when he was very young, which broke Lucy's heart.

I am an Anne of Green Gables fan, so when I first read about the writer's sad life and multiple losses, I was surprised she was able to write her tales of Anne with such spunk and verve. I find it amazing that a woman who had every reason to be melancholy wrote books that have circled the globe, delighting children and adults alike with its charm and wit. Lucy was developed by her sorrows; otherwise, I don't think she would have been able to pen twenty such uplifting books.

People who know my husband, Les, are amazed that he had an abusive father. Les is kind, thoughtful, helpful, humorous, and generous, as well as a supportive dad and a tender grandfather. Les is everything his father never was. Some of those qualities he learned by watching his mom, but some of them were forged in his hostile environment. Les knew he never wanted to be like his dad, so he searched for a better way, a higher path.

There's something about loss that has the potential to take us by the hand and help us find a way to survive outside the context of our pain.

I have found that my mistakes often lead to a clearer resolve, my losses often bulldoze a path to untapped courage, and my limitations can teach internal liberty by God's grace.

"Therefore we do not lose heart. Even though our outward man is perishing, yet the inward man is being renewed day by day. For our light affliction, which is but for a moment, is working for us a far more exceeding and eternal weight of glory" (2 Corinthians 4:16–17 NIV).

Don't allow crusty old frogs along your path to throw you. Butterflies are just around the corner.

God, help me not to be discouraged by the "petrified frogs" in my life. Give me an eternal perspective on my circumstances today, knowing that nothing is going to be perfect until heaven.

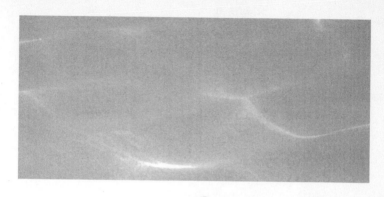

Freedom To...

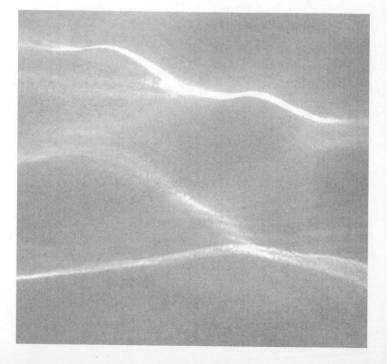

Freedom to Believe the Truth

Mary Graham

You shall know the truth, and the
truth shall make you free.

—John 8:32 NKJV

Sometimes I'm amazed at how easily I believe. I've never considered myself very gullible or naive, but maybe I am. For instance, when I go to the makeup counter at my local department store and ask for a refill on a jar of foundation, if the woman says to me, "Oh my goodness. Are you not layering your makeup? You need lotion, primer, and crème," I believe her. The next thing I know, I'm walking out the door with a bag of stuff so I can layer my makeup.

And then there's Bailey. Bailey is my adorable dog who, quite frankly, lies to me regularly. When he wants a treat and I remind him he's already had one, he looks at me in disgust. He looks at me so forlornly that I end up believing his lie and giving him yet another treat.

I believe stuff every day that is not even close to the truth. Interestingly, however, what I know to be true, I often find myself doubting.

The first time I remember hearing the gospel was when I was a junior in college. Even though I'd been a part of a local church all my life, somehow the reality of personal faith in Christ had escaped me. Faith was something to believe in, not necessarily something to live by. That having a personal relationship with the God of the Bible was possible for someone like me seemed very hard to embrace.

But a wonderful woman—whose name, incidentally, was Faith—took me under her wing and began to teach me from the Word of God. To be honest, what she taught struck me not as the truth but more like wishful thinking. Was it possible that God loved me? Sent his Son to die for me? Extended to me love, grace, and forgiveness for my sins? Could I believe that he created me, knew all the details of my life, and accepted me just as I was? Was it true that I was special to him? That I was uniquely and wonderfully made? That he loved me as if there were no one else to love?

All of that and more, Faith assured me, was the truth. Not because she said so but because it's what the Bible teaches. I, along with hundreds of other college students, sat under the tutelage of Faith and her husband, Cal, for the next three years until I joined the staff of Campus Crusade for Christ. Apart from what they taught me and how they literally poured their lives into mine, I would never have been prepared for any kind of ministry. Their time with me was one of the hallmarks of my life.

Nonetheless, it took a long time for me to completely embrace the truth. I heard what they were saying, I read it for myself, and I sensed changes in my life both outwardly and inwardly. I knew I had a new power from within that enabled me to make better choices. But there were times I would still ask, "Is this true?"

I had to come to the place in my life where, by faith, I could take God at his Word. Billy Graham tells the story of coming to that same place. He never experienced freedom until he proclaimed to God and to the world that he would believe the Bible as the Word of God. I've heard him tell that story many times because it was the turning point in his life.

Jesus said, "You shall know the truth, and the truth shall make you free" (John 8:32 NKJV). For many years, I didn't know the truth, but since I've known, it has been a process to embrace and experience the freedom it brings.

Freedom is hard to come by, and I know very few people who actually enjoy it. But those who do enjoy true freedom have something in common: they've learned to take God at his Word, regardless of what they think or feel. They understand knowing what God says is valid and undeniable no matter what.

Ney Bailey is the person I know best who talks about this most. Her book, *Faith Is Not a Feeling*, expresses the freedom of true faith in the most easily understood way.[2] Ney has served all over the world in a ministry helping people understand that trusting God has everything to do with believing that what he says is true.

Ney and I have shared a home for many years and have been involved in ministry together hundreds of times through the years. Regarding issues of life, whether huge or seemingly insignificant, she demonstrates simple faith. She knows what the Scripture says, she believes it to be true, and it changes everything for her. She's free to pursue life in all its fullness because of this foundation of truth.

I learn the same thing from Luci Swindoll, who is my opposite in temperament and personality. Luci and I became friends in the mid-1970s. It didn't take me long to see her very strong faith in God and his Word. She demonstrated that faith was her most dependable reality. Luci grew up with parents and grandparents who were men and women of faith. By the time she was a young adult, she was engaged in very serious study of the Bible. She learned the basic doctrines of Christian faith and internalized them deeply and with great conviction. Through the years, I've observed in Luci a steadfast, immovable faith that leaves no room for doubt.

The first chapter of James, verses two through six, perfectly describes Luci's life: "My brethren, count it all joy when you fall into various trials, knowing that the testing of your faith produces patience. But let patience have its perfect work, that you may be perfect and complete, lacking nothing. If any of you lacks wisdom, let him ask of God, who gives to all liberally and without reproach, and it will be given to him. But let him ask in faith, with no doubting, for he who doubts is like a wave of the sea driven and tossed by the wind" (NKJV).

Luci is a picture of stability, and I believe it's because she holds on to the truth without wavering. The truth has set her free.

When I'd only known Luci a few months, she invited me to come to church with her. She mentioned that her brother was her pastor and that we'd need to go very early in order to obtain seats for one of the five services. I wondered, *Who in the world is your brother?* That morning, thirty years ago, I walked into Luci's church and heard her little brother, Chuck Swindoll, teach from the book of Acts. I had never heard more wonderful, compelling, crystal-clear teaching in my life. From that day until this, Luci's brother has been my Bible teacher. For the second time in my life, thankfully, I live in a city where Chuck pastors a church. Sunday mornings are like being someone's guest at the most delightful dinner party in town: it's a feast, full of life and nurture for my soul.

If I get home early on Sunday morning from a trip, I drop off my bags and race to church. If I fly in at midnight on Saturday night, it doesn't matter how tired I feel; I don't miss church. Not because I can't, but because I don't want to.

Chuck presents the truth, and I starve without it. The truth that sets me free is elusive for me, and I need to be reminded of it all the time. There's no better reminder for me than Chuck's Bible teaching, whether I hear him in person, on tape, on the radio—or read his teaching in a book. Everybody needs a good Bible teacher, and he is mine.

The woman at the makeup counter has an agenda. She wants to sell more makeup so she can make more money. She likely is not truly concerned about whether I leave the house on any given day without my makeup layered. My dog, Bailey, certainly has an agenda. He wants treats, and his plan is to connive as many out of me as possible.

The truth isn't part of everyone's agenda. But for me, I am bound to the constraints of my own limited mind and fragile emotional state if I don't hang on to the truth of the Word of God with my whole heart. Only then am I free indeed.

Father God, today I will take you at your Word, regardless of what I think or feel. Help me experience the freedom that comes from clinging to your truth.

Freedom to Trust God's Plan

Barbara Johnson

Let the morning bring me word of your unfailing
love, for I have put my trust in you. Show me the
way I should go, for to you I lift up my soul.

—Psalm 143:8 NIV

*B*efore cancer took away my freedom to travel, I thought nothing of flitting all over the country to "spread my joy," as I liked to say. Coast-to-coast flights and complicated schedules were commonplace, but thanks to my husband, Bill, who loved to keep us organized and moving according to plan, we were almost always on time and in the right place.

Whenever we did find ourselves in the wrong place, it was almost always someone else's fault—like the time the airport driver was supposed to drop us off at the Marriott but instead unloaded us at the Hyatt. He had been hired by the group that was hosting my speaking engagement, and all we knew was that he was taking us to our hotel. We didn't know which hotel it was—and didn't discover his error until we tried to check in and the registration clerk had no reservations for us. But eventually we were able to contact our hosts, get ourselves to the right hotel, and return to the original plan.

Another time, I thought I was simply meeting someone for lunch (a prize she had won in a contest sponsored by a bookstore somewhere). But when I got there, I found out she had invited about a hundred of her "closest friends" to join us, and I was asked to give a speech! Of course I was happy to do so; I just regretted that I hadn't known what the plan included, so I hadn't brought along any of my props.

I always knew what city we were going to and (usually) knew what kind of presentation I was expected to give when I got there, but I didn't always know the details of every trip's plan as we left home. But that was okay. I just needed to know where I was going and who was in charge, and the rest . . . well, I let someone else worry about that and simply followed the steps Bill or the event organizers laid out for me.

When something went wrong, it might have been frustrating for a little while; but in the end, the quirks or kinks that developed in the plan usually gave me a funny story to share. Being gifted with a bubble of joy, I was usually able to laugh about whatever kind of *I Love Lucy* calamity we found ourselves in. (On the other hand, Bill, a former shipshape navy officer, had a hard time seeing the humor in the situation whenever the plan wasn't followed exactly.)

There's usually an upside and a downside to just about everything that happens to us. One of my friends insists that God created the world with balance in mind, and she uses my travel experiences as an example. "Barb, whenever something bad happened—when the plane was delayed or the car broke down or you got lost in the tunnels of the big arena just before you were to speak—think about what else happened during that time," she said. "You met someone really interesting while you were waiting for the plane, or some Good Samaritan stopped on the freeway to help fix your car, or you came upon that little sign in the tunnel that made you laugh. Remember? It said, 'If you are reading this, you've gone way too far.' Through your experiences and through my own, I've learned that when something bad happens, I have to be patient. I have to hang on. Something good will happen soon. God's got a plan, and that plan has a happy ending."

Her words remind me of another friend's story about a long-ago disappointment during high school. At her small, rural high school, cheerleaders for the basketball team were elected by a vote of the student population. She'd been on the squad the previous two years, so it was especially hard when her junior year began and she wasn't reelected. The election took place in the morning, and she had a hard time enduring the rest of that long, sad school day, her young heart broken as she felt her fellow students' rejection and thought of all the fun she would be missing the next year as her friends carried on with their enthusiastic cheerleading.

Finally, the last class ended and she hurried home to be alone. She went to her favorite secret spot on a secluded hillside below her family's home and let the tears flow. As she sat there, weeping, she heard footsteps and then saw her father making his way down the steep trail. She was startled to see him, surprised that he had left work early and amazed that he knew where to find her.

Somehow he'd found out what happened at school that day. But he never mentioned it. He sat down beside her, idly plucked a tall blade of grass, and said, "I was just thinking. You'll be sixteen soon. It's time you learned how to drive. Would you like me to give you a driving lesson today?"

Of course she would! As one of the youngest students in her class, she'd watched with envy as friends had already turned sixteen and experienced the freedom of being able to drive themselves wherever they needed to go around town. She and her dad quickly walked back up the trail, climbed into the family car, and headed for a field on the family farm where the day that had begun so miserably ended with a happy sense of adventure and accomplishment. Something good had balanced out the bad.

But the next day at school, reality returned, and she couldn't help but feel sad again, thinking that her friends would soon be swept up in the basketball team's quest for the championship. Then, at lunchtime, the basketball coach asked her if she would be the team's statistician during the coming season. She quickly agreed.

Her new position meant she still got to ride the bus with the cheerleaders and basketball players to all the games, and, she said, "I got lots more attention from the boys on the team when I was statistician than I ever had as cheerleader, because the players always wanted to know their stats. I had to keep track of every shot attempted—where it was made from and whether the shot was good—and I had to figure percentages for each player, how many field goals or free throws were attempted, and how many were made. So suddenly all the boys on the team were always wanting to talk to me!"

The experience was a life lesson for that young woman. It taught her to look for something good in the difficult experiences that have come her way since then, knowing that God's plan is to prosper her and to give her hope. It reminded her that even when setbacks and challenges occur, she must be patient and wait for the next step of the plan to unfold.

In a strange but marvelous way, her belief gives her a sense of freedom because she knows she doesn't have to figure out the big picture by herself. She doesn't have to see how each piece of her life fits into God's big, glorious picture. She just keeps believing. Keeps praying. Keeps trusting. And she knows that in the end, God's plan will be revealed to her, and she'll be able to see her life as God sees it. So in the darkness, she watches for a flame of hope to appear; when she feels lost, she waits for a new door of opportunity to open.

Since cancer took away my good health, I've experienced many moments of darkness, many losses. One of the hardest has been my loss of mobility—my freedom to *go*. At first, I was no longer able to travel around the country; I couldn't fly. What a loss that was, to give up the travel I had enjoyed so much!

Then, after a while, my doctor recommended that I no longer drive. That was a blow, too, but it was bearable because Bill could drive me where I needed to go.

Then Bill died. Since then, I've had to depend on the kindness of others for transportation, and most of my travel revolves around medical appointments—with an occasional outing to Marie Callender's for pie à la mode with my friends.

Gradually, my world has shrunk from a coast-to-coast map to the walls of my home. To be honest, I'm still waiting for the good thing that will balance out the losses I've had to accept since my illness began six years ago. I'm not sure that particular "good thing" will occur this side of heaven. But I know it *will* happen, either here or there. And I'm going to keep on believing, keep on praying, and keep on trusting the One who blessed me so long ago with a bubble of joy that keeps my spirits high even when things go wrong.

For years, one of my lifelines has been the statement Job made as he, too, was beset by challenges: "Though he slay me, yet will I trust in him" (13:15a KJV). As one of my friends likes to say, "Ain't nothin' gonna change that now."

I don't have to figure out *why* or *how* or *when.* God has a plan, and I'm committed to it. That commitment frees me from having to worry about the details. I just need to know where I'm going and who's in charge. And believe me, now more than ever, I do!

———

Lord, help me remember that I don't have to figure out the big picture by myself. I'll just keep believing, praying, and trusting you, knowing that you have a great plan for me!

Freedom to Love One Another

Nicole Johnson

Owe no one anything except to love one another,
for he who loves another has fulfilled the law.

—Romans 13:8 NKJV

My family is celebrating my parents' twenty-fifth anniversary this year. Many families have done this kind of celebration for generations, but I'd like to tell you why it's incredibly special for us. You'll catch on right away, as I lay out the complications.

My mother, Leah (a mother of three), married David, my stepfather, when I was fourteen. David had two children, a son and a daughter, and with my sister and half-brother we totaled five kids. Our parents married amid controversy and difficulty—my brother was serving our country in the air force, and my new stepsister had gone to South Africa to live with her mother. My new stepbrother was graduating from high school and joining the air force, where he would serve in Indonesia and then Australia. My sister had made the hard decision at that time to live with our father in Alabama. So when my mother and stepfather married in May 1981, by August of that year, all my brothers and sisters—halfs, steps, and wholes— were gone. And I, the baby of the family, lived at home alone for another three years until I went away to college.

Now here is why my parents' anniversary celebration is so unbelievably remarkable: our family has remained just as spread out, if not more so, for the last twenty-five years. It was as if we all got blown to the ends of the earth. Today finds us in Texas, Australia, Ireland, Louisiana, California, and Alabama. For these reasons and others, family visits have always been with one or two siblings at a time. Since our parents' marriage, and even before to the very best of my recollection, my siblings and parents have never all been together in the same room at one time. Not once did everyone come home for Christmas. We haven't gathered as a family to celebrate anything—until now. And the only thing that has brought us together, though we are all different, and dare I say wonderful, is love. Our parents have demonstrated a steady and consistent love for each other and for each of us over the last twenty-five years, and now it is drawing us all together, freely, by our love for them.

Through these years, each of us has been on a journey. Some have grown in faith and some have grown stronger emotionally, but we have all grown in our freedom to love each other. This is made plain by the fact that no one is being forced to come to this celebration. In fact, any one of us could have come up with legitimate reasons to stay home. All of us siblings have responsibilities and families of our own. All of us have to travel—some farther than others—but no one lives close. Each of us will sacrifice to make the trip because we are finally free after all these years, after all the pain, after all the breaks, to come together as one family under our parents and their twenty-five-year love.

This is indeed amazing freedom. As you might guess, it hasn't always been this way for our family. We've had very real hurts and disappointments; many we thought might never be mended. We were plenty free *not* to get together for our parents' anniversary, but the harder-fought freedom was to come home in our hearts long enough to surround our parents with honor and love.

Love sets us free, and then we are set free to love one another—that's not a cliché; it's a deep and profound truth. In healthy families, this happens naturally from parents to the child and then from the child to others and back to the parents. In families that are broken apart, it still can happen, but it often takes much more time and love to bring all the pieces back together. Time is an amazing healer, but it is not only time. Time can soften a rock in a riverbed or turn a living tree into stone. It is the abiding presence of love that determines what time will produce in our hearts.

When we are deeply loved, we have the greatest freedom known to man. Love gives us wings and lets us take flight. It is this freedom that a life journey with Christ produces in us. It's not that after years of walking with God we feel we are "better"; hopefully, we are freer. We are set free to pour out love and grace and mercy on others out of the abundant supply of love that is given freely to us.

And we can see the contrast. People who do not know love in the core of their being are stingy in their hearts. They seek to hoard the little love that they have for fear it will be taken away from them. In actuality, the reverse is true. Love shrinks in response to hoarding and fear, which in turn multiplies the mistrust and anxiety.

But to allow the love of God to take hold of us and to possess our hearts with its strength and beauty is to unlock the prison of fear and usher us into the freedom of being able to love others. We are no longer poor; we are no longer paupers with nothing to offer. We have been given the riches of heaven, and we are free to live like kings, lavishing love and care on all those around us.

Soon our formerly wounded and scattered clan will be living like a royal family. Robed in the luxurious love of our parents, who have journeyed far in their own faith, and feasting at the table of grace and forgiveness, we will celebrate that out of the ashes of loneliness, poor choices, and chaos, a beautiful love has emerged. Refined by the fire of difficulties and trials, standing tall by the strength of faith commitment, it is shining as bright as gold reflecting in the sun. So many of the former impurities are gone forever, proving to us all what we have hoped for—that love really does set us free.

———

Father, for your love we are more grateful than we can ever express. We humbly ask you to help your love set us free that we may be bigger in our hearts, kinder to those around us, more forgiving of those who hurt us, and more loving to all who know us. Set us free to be more like you.

Freedom to Have Abundant Life

Thelma Wells

> The thief does not come except to steal,
> and to kill, and to destroy.
> I have come that they may have life, and that
> they may have it more abundantly.
>
> —John 10:10 NKJV

During the first week of July 2005, I had the time of my life. It was the most joyous, fun-filled, tiring five days I've had in decades. It was the first time I had the blessing of getting all my grandchildren and my great-granddaughter together at our cabin in Texas.

I went to the lake house early to prepare for everybody's coming. I bought lots of supplies and was convinced I got all I needed for the next several days.

Little did I realize how much food children could consume in a day's time! The milk, fruit, chips, bread, juice, ham, cheese, and bottled water floated away in their little (or big?) stomachs faster than a woodchuck chucking wood. It's probably because they ran and played, screamed and yelled, swam and sprinkled themselves with the water hose, stepped in ants, got stung by mosquitoes, were pierced by sticker buds, caught baby frogs from sunup to sunset, and watched DVDs only when they were about to collapse into a sleep coma.

All the while, I was watching them, cooking for them, cleaning up after them, and washing, drying, folding, and putting away their laundry—only to have to do it again thirty minutes later. Oh the joys of being a grandmother! I was totally exhausted but thrilled to goodness they were there. We had a fantastic time together.

Now I'm not comparing myself with God, but I thought about him a lot as I took care of my grandchildren. I thought about how he has prepared our daily bread and spread a table before us. What blessings he bestows! I thought about how he quenches our thirst every day and gives us living water that cannot be found in a store or a well but from the riches of his storehouse of love.

I can just imagine how God looks down and chuckles when he sees us enjoying the people and things he has provided for us on this earth. Can you just see him smiling as Adam named the animals—especially when Adam came up with names like *orangutan* or *octopus*? Can you see him looking at Adam and Eve in the Garden of Eden and laughing with them when they were kidding each other?

In John 10:10, Jesus declares that he came to earth that we

may have life and that we may have it more abundantly. This Scripture bothered me for a long time. Well, not the entire Scripture but the part about *more abundantly*. I wondered what that meant. More abundantly than what?

One day I started discussing John 10:10 with some friends, and I finally got my answer. Jesus' coming was not to spare us from the difficult things of life. That lesson has to be learned in Real Life 101. But he came to free our spirits from bottling up our hurts and pain and putting them in the warehouse of our minds forever. He knew that if we kept all the bad stuff that happened to us in that storage place, we would never be able to really enjoy life to its fullest. The ghosts of the past and the gall of the present would diminish our future pleasures.

Jesus knows that it is not what happens to us on the outside that causes depression, oppression, and distress; it's how we respond to it on the inside. Therefore, he came to set our spirits free so we could enjoy everything he has created for us. Hallelujah!

What is abundant life? Let me share with you a letter from my friend "Precious" that may help us understand it.

> After I had an abortion, I sank into a pit of despair and regret, and my life became a control game. In 1996, I came to the end of myself and surrendered my heart and life to the Lord Jesus Christ. For the first time ever,

I saw just how much I was loved. As I grew in my faith and trust, I gave the Lord more and more of the things that were standing in the way, keeping me from an abundant life.

When I was eleven, I started to embrace a very dangerous eating disorder as my best friend. For the next twenty-five years, that little friend would go from being a huge giant to sometimes a closet hider, but I always knew just where to find my friend when I needed to control things.

After coming to know Jesus, I left my friend in the closet for a while and only pulled her out when I needed to. The problem was that because of my abortion, I had gained more than one hundred pounds trying to "feed the hurt." Anorexic behavior quickly turned into bulimic behavior, and my weight took a mad roller-coaster ride. I went from fat clothes to skinny clothes about twenty times during the years to come. Yet I would never pull my friend out of the closet long enough to introduce her to anyone who cared about me.

About two years ago, I was at a meeting when the time came to make introductions. My close friends had been watching me and sat down in a hotel room to talk with me about my "closet friend." I saw that I would have to sever that friendship now that she knew others in my life. After returning home, I called my doctor and asked for some help. I put that friend way in the back of the closet and shut that door, praying that her absence would make others believe in me.

Over the next two years, I did a fairly good job of keeping bulimia out of my life. The Lord began to bless me in many ways. I had chances to meet and speak to people and watch lives change. Good things were becoming abundant in my daily life. I can't figure out just why my "friend" remained in my home . . . but she did. Even though I spent less time with her, I just couldn't put her completely out of my life. I spent a lot of effort to make sure that no one talked to her or saw me play with her when she would come out of my closet, not really realizing that God was watching.

This weekend [at the Women of Faith conference], the Lord spoke truth to me about my friend. More than once I heard that as long as I was in control, God wasn't. I am so stubborn! I just wanted to hang onto my friend's hand, but I knew that if I did, holding a firm grip on the Lord would be impossible.

I took a drive with my friend Wonderful yesterday. She pulled over on a country road at a small cement bridge and asked me to take a walk. I had been so wrapped up knowing I was going to have to ditch my friend in the closet that I let my guard down long enough for someone to see inside my pain.

As Wonderful and I walked out onto the bridge, we began to talk about things. I found myself pouring out my struggles. Then Wonderful said something that finally clicked with me. She said, "Precious, I do not understand the pains of this, but I do know that you can trust our God." I knew for the first time ever that was the truth of it all. I have struggled for so long, too long. I cannot have what is God's already. He bought me with a price. I am not mine, and to have control is not even a possibility.

I made a decision to leave my friend on the bridge yesterday. Wonderful and I prayed before driving away without her. The Lord has put her away for me because I did not have the strength to walk in freedom as long as she stayed in my home. I went back home without her, and it just doesn't feel so scary to me anymore.

I am not afraid to fly away without my friend because I know in my heart that the best is yet to come—God's abundance promised in John 10:10.

Precious now has the freedom to enjoy life more abundantly. Are *you* taking advantage of your amazing freedom to enjoy life at its fullest?

We can be free to have abundant life when we trust God and allow him to wash our dirty laundry and clean up our mess. When we come to him, he forgives us and allows us another chance to stay clean. He never gets tired of our screaming, yelling, running, hurting, and crying. He just listens to us, holds us close, and puts his loving balm on the bites of life.

Whenever we want to enjoy the abundant life God has given us, we can gladly surrender our lives to him, knowing, like Precious, that "the best is yet to come"!

———

Father God, help me today to experience the amazing freedom and abundant life that you have given me.

Freedom to Hope During Trials

Patsy Clairmont

Shall we indeed accept good from God,
and shall we not accept adversity?

—Job 2:10 NKJV

I was sitting in my office doing a typing assignment in my usual hunt-and-peck style, while my husband, Les, was nestled in the family room in his favorite comfy chair working a crossword puzzle, when it happened. (Have you noticed that life's happenings are usually intruders—bullies in boots?) It had been a normal morning on a sunny day when there was a sudden, thunderous *bam*!

Startled, I called to Les, "What in the world was that?"

"I don't know," he answered, bewildered.

"It sounded like an eagle hit a window," I quipped sarcastically.

"Come here, Patsy," Les called calmly, the type of "calmly" that makes you sprint to see what's up. I hurried into the family room, and there was my baffled husband pointing to the top of our window. I followed Les's gaze—and what I saw shook the vocabulary out of me. Not an easy thing to do, I might add. What I saw was a bullet hole. Uh-huh, a *bullet hole*, as in a hole created by a projectile that is ejected out of a gun barrel. Someone had shot a bullet through our window about nine feet above my husband's head.

Now nine feet is a lot if you're trying to, say, reach up and change a light bulb, if you're facing a giant opponent in a boxing ring, or when you're in a checkout lane and in a hurry; but when it's a bullet shot over the head of your husband, nine feet is way too close! Trust me, emotionally, that bullet felt like it left skid marks on Les's thinning hair and my last, splintered nerve.

We immediately called the police and filed a report, but for the life of us we couldn't figure out where the shot could have come from. We have neighbors all around us, but we saw no one. Many of the abodes close to ours are often not even occupied. We live in a quiet circle of homes, which made the incident more mysterious.

When the police officer arrived and viewed the entry point, he concluded it was from a high-powered pellet gun. The word *pellet* made me feel a little better . . . although *high-powered* made me feel a lot worse.

That evening, we (okay, me) were initially reluctant to sit in the family room since we didn't know who the shooter was or what he was shooting at. We (okay, me) found ourselves uncertain exactly where in our windowed home was safe for us to sit, which created an uneasy evening for us (okay, me). I kept glancing up at the entry point and wondering if the shooter would return.

The next day, the mystery was solved when a sheepish neighbor (no, he wasn't a teenager) came and confessed he was shooting at a squirrel and missed.

He may have missed the squirrel, but he did hit the target of our jangled nerves—bull's-eye! There's just something about a bullet, even a stray one, that is utterly unsettling, especially when it strays into your personal space. You read about those things happening on the news, but you don't expect it in your neighborhood and especially not at your home.

This jarring incident reinforced to me that we don't know what a day will bring. We live a life of surprises. We may not have a clue that life is about to take a careening left turn. Everything may seem usual, when suddenly a high-powered crisis hits us broadside—*bam*! And nothing in the landscape of our lives ever looks quite the same again.

In our case, all we had to do was replace the window and settle down (yes, me). Trust me, replacing Les would have been much harder since his model number has been out of stock for years.

My friend, though, was not as fortunate when crisis slammed into her life. She thought her husband would always be with her, at least through retirement years or until one sat graveside at the other's interment. Why wouldn't she? They'd been married for more than thirty years. But one day he decided to push his shopping cart down a new aisle, leaving her in the checkout lane to pay the high cost of grief. His leaving made no sense to her, their children, or friends. But sense or not, he's gone—and her heart is crushed and her future has changed dramatically.

Will my friend recover? Absolutely. Will their children adjust? Eventually. Will the husband ever regret his choice? Possibly.

Loss opens us up to vengeance or victory, depending on our ability to let go of our rights. Quite honestly, this life will never be right. It is under the dominating infiltration of the enemy, who breeds wrong. He slings evil around like confetti on a parade, and he celebrates our pain as he taunts us from the lofty float of his own sick agenda. And until his ultimate demise, we will often feel blindsided.

But we are not without hope during trials. I have seen the radiance of those who have won freedom from the enemy's grasp, I have heard their hope-filled insights birthed out of their despair, and I have inspected their tangible faith as it glistened like gold out of the furnace of affliction.

Consider Job. He had a machine-gun spray of problems hit all at once. Through the window of his life came multiple "bullets" aimed at his heart. And it is from him that we hear these costly words: "Shall we indeed accept good from God, and shall we not accept adversity?" (Job 2:10 NKJV).

Job lost his oxen and donkeys to marauders, his servants at the site were murdered, his sheep and servants at another pasture were burned by a fire that fell out of the sky, then his camels were stolen and those servants killed, and as if all that was not enough for one heart to bear, word arrived that the house where all of his grown children were eating together had collapsed and none had survived.

How does one bear that kind of multiple loss?

I think if I can understand why something happens it would help, but when you've lost your children (or child), there is no answer that is reasonable or satisfactory to a parent's heart.

As Job clamored around, shackled by shock and chained to grief, a frantic prisoner searching for a way out, he stumbled into relinquishment. In essence, he admitted, who are we to determine our destiny? Who are we to counsel God? Who are we to try to reason with the holy?

Our freedom comes during life's inequities as we fall into the arms of God's sovereign plan. The saying "Let go and let God," while it may sound trite in the midst of troubles, is actually sound theology. The Lord has a high plan he is executing even in the injustices of our lives, and while the plan unfolds, he tends to us.

"The Spirit of the Sovereign LORD ... has sent me to bind up the brokenhearted, to proclaim freedom for the captives and release from darkness for the prisoners" (Isaiah 61:1–2 NIV).

There is comfort and hope in the fact that God has placed eternity into the heart of man, and then through Christ, God has given us access to it. We know what we experience here is not the whole story but instead is the prelude; yet here and now is all we've known, so it's sometimes hard to imagine the beyond. We feel the tug of eternity in our hearts, but we have a hard time wrapping our understanding around the ethereal. Perhaps that is why we are given a preview of things to come in the book of Revelation . . . to keep us pressing on during difficult times.

If you have suffered a recent calamity, may these words part the seas of your grief long enough to give you a vision of our coming freedom that will enable you to hope during trials.

> Then I saw a new heaven and a new earth, for the first heaven and the first earth had passed away, and there was no longer any sea. I saw the Holy City, the new Jerusalem, coming down out of heaven from God, prepared as a bride beautifully dressed for her husband. And I heard a loud voice from the throne saying, "Now the dwelling of God is with men, and he will live with them. They will be his people, and God himself will be with them and be their God. He will wipe every tear from their eyes. There will be no more death or mourning,

or crying, for the old order of things has passed away."
(Revelation 21:1–4 NIV)

I don't know what is going on in your corner of the world, but I know the One who does. Christ is in the midst of disaster, death, and gratefully even the smallest details of our unfolding lives.

We who have invited Christ into our war-worn hearts are never, never, no never alone. And that, my friend, spells *f-r-e-e-d-o-m*, no matter what our shell-shocked situation may be.

Whew!

———

God, it's so hard to find hope in my earthly trials! Comfort me today, and give me the strength to keep pressing on as I trust in your promise of my eternal freedom.

Freedom to Be Kind

Marilyn Meberg

Be kind to one another.

—Ephesians 4:32a NKJV

*W*ell now, isn't that kind?" was a statement Mrs. Hooker frequently made. She lived next door to us when I was seven years old. She smiled a lot, made me lemonade, and told me I was kind. Naturally, I liked her. Because I was sure she was at least 128 years old, I felt constrained to do "kind" things for her each day because I was certain she had only few days left. I wanted her remaining time on earth to be filled with good things. (I was such a precious child . . .)

One day we were sitting on Mrs. Hooker's front porch drinking lemonade. I was chattering on endlessly about my wildly exciting life when Mrs. Hooker interjected, "Well now, isn't that kind?" at a moment that didn't fit. I'd been describing how John Dietz kept poking Darlene Partridge in the ribs during reading group that morning. That Mrs. Hooker should say John's behavior was kind startled me. I looked at her face to see if her expression would help me understand why she said what she did. But she continued to smile and encouraged me to keep talking.

With the passing of time and many porch conversations under my belt, I realized Mrs. Hooker frequently said, "Well now, isn't that kind?" when the comment didn't fit. I was alarmed to ultimately realize Mrs. Hooker didn't have a clue about what was kind and what was not. In fact, sadly, I realized Mrs. Hooker didn't really have a clue about much of anything. She was pleasant, made good lemonade, and encouraged my chatter, but I began to find our times together troubling. My mother encouraged me to continue my kindnesses to Mrs. Hooker but to understand that her mind was not as sharp as it once was and advised me to not take it personally when she had a fadeout that produced a "Well now, isn't that kind?" comment that didn't fit.

Reluctantly, I got used to this new reality about Mrs. Hooker. When her neighbor's dog chased a frantic cat up a tree and Mrs. Hooker said, "Well now, isn't that kind?" her words fell into a new category in my thinking, but things were never the same for me. I wanted her to really know that dog was wrong to chase a cat up the tree. I wanted Mrs. Hooker to know the difference between kind and unkind. And, of course, I wanted her to know I truly was kind.

The dictionary defines *kind* as exhibiting a "friendly, generous, and warmhearted nature." We all love people who display a generous and warmhearted nature. Such people make us feel secure and safe. Such people cause us to believe in the possibility of a world with only porches and lemonade instead of mean dogs and scared cats.

I have recently become the recipient of behavior that is truly "friendly, generous, and warmhearted" from my good friend Les Clairmont. Not long ago, while he and Patsy were driving home from the mall, Les said, "Patsy, I want to do something really nice for Marilyn, but I don't know what that could be."

I had just had back surgery that I thought would immediately eliminate my nerve pain; it did not. (Now, three weeks later, the pain is steadily decreasing, but for a while I feared I'd have to learn how to manage that pain the rest of my life.) Les commented to Patsy that my house was full of flowers from dear friends cheering me on, so he knew I was certainly not in need of another bouquet. "What do you think I could do?"

After thoughtful reflection, Patsy said, "Well, she's not eating much; the pain has really diminished her appetite. I know she loves custard, and I think that would be soothing for her. But where can you buy custard that doesn't come in a little Gerber jar from the grocery store?"

"I know how to get good custard, Patsy," Les said. "I am going to make her some."

Patsy stared at her husband in disbelief. "You've never made custard in your life, Leslie Clairmont!"

"I know, but it's time I started!"

As soon as they got home, Patsy scoured her cookbooks for a custard recipe but couldn't find one. They called a friend in Michigan who did not have one either. Finally, Patsy found a custard recipe on the Internet and copied it down. With the recipe in hand, Les went to the grocery store and bought each item, including perfect little custard cups. Then, according to Patsy, he threw himself into clattering and banging around the kitchen. Several hours later, he sent Patsy to my house bearing warm-from-the-oven custard. I was stunned when Patsy walked in with these treasures. "Did you do this, Patsy? How kind!" I said.

"I'd love to take credit, but Les did these himself," Patsy admitted. "You have to know, Marilyn, this is from a guy who never cooks except to occasionally throw a hunk of cow on the barbecue. I can't guarantee this offering."

I sat down and dove immediately into the first little cup. It was fantastic! Then I dove into the second little cup . . . equally fantastic. What a wonderfully soothing and satisfying treat! Patsy stared at me as I shamelessly devoured all the custard. She said, "You know, Marilyn, custard is one of my favorite foods too. I can't believe I've been married to Les Clairmont for more than forty years and had no idea I could have been crying out for custard all that time!" Of course, I'm encouraging Patsy not to be bitter.

Now, two weeks later, Patsy regularly comes to my door with warm-from-the-oven custard from "the custard man." I am thrilled and grateful. With a full heart and contented stomach, I have to say, "Well now, isn't that kind?"

Second Peter speaks of the righteousness of God and how we are to mirror that righteousness to others. These words describe what Les is doing for me: "Now for this very reason also, applying all diligence, in your faith supply moral excellence, and in your moral excellence, knowledge; and in your knowledge, self-control, and in your self-control, perseverance, and in your perseverance, godliness; and in your godliness, brotherly kindness" (1:5–7 NASB). Thanks, Les, for your brotherly kindness.

There is real freedom we experience as we live out of a heart of intentional kindness. When I was attempting to make Mrs. Hooker's life pleasant, I felt a sense of *This is right . . . this is good,* which translated into a sense of peace for my seven-year-old soul. Now, admittedly, I had the human urge to get credit and to be recognized as a kind little kid, but that self-serving tendency was not the source of my gratification. The source of gratification came from responding to God's directive about how I was to live.

The theology of that was not yet clear to me, but the inner feeling was. The Holy Spirit took up residence in me when I was five years old. I learned that as a result of his presence I was compelled to do the right thing and was uncomfortable when I didn't. One of the verses I learned in Sunday school was "Be kind to one another" (Ephesians 4:32 NKJV). No matter how that verse might cramp my style, I knew when I paid attention to it and obeyed, there came with that obedience a sense of inner freedom.

First Corinthians 13:4 says, "Love suffers long and is kind" (NKJV). That comes with the same freedom-producing reward. I have learned over the years that my job as a believer in and receiver of Jesus as my Savior is to be obedient to his admonitions. With that obedience comes a lightness of being that I recognize as freedom from the shackles of selfish self-centeredness.

It is interesting to observe the outpouring of kindness and love from thousands of people responding to the enormous needs of those whose lives have recently been devastated by floods, hurricanes, tornados, tsunamis, and earthquakes. People from all over the world are responding quickly and generously in an effort to rebuild homes, restore health, and reunite loved ones. This outpouring of human caring springs from people who do not necessarily know Christ as Savior. But they do know that the urging in their hearts to help and be kind cannot be ignored. Where does that urging come from?

We are all created in the image of God. We each bear the indelible God-imprint that unites us as persons created by God. One of the characteristics of God is that he is a God of love. He is a God who is kind and promises to meet us in our need no matter how large or small. That God-imprint is carried by all persons. Some have chosen to go against it and refuse to acknowledge that all human beings are to be treated with love and kindness. Then there are some who choose to live out of their God-given desire to be kind but do not choose to receive Christ as Savior. Those persons miss the joy of being personally connected to the very One who authors their instinct to be kind. God placed that instinct within all people. What we do with it is a choice each of us is free to make.

As believers, we hear the words of Jesus, who told the disciples as well as those of us who follow centuries later to "give as freely as you have received" (Matthew 10:8 NLT). Our acts of kindness spring from gratitude toward God, who has given to us freely. Each of us experiences soul freedom as we give.

Although Mrs. Hooker lost the ability to discern what was kind and what was not, she nevertheless continued to give freely to me. Her porch and her lemonade were always available. So now, nearly sixty years later, I can look back on her daily receiving of me and say, "Well now, wasn't that kind?"

———

Lord, reveal to me how I can intentionally show kindness to others. Release me from the bondage of self-centeredness so I can freely give to others as I have received from you.

Freedom to Have Fun

Luci Swindoll

Friend, you have no idea how good your love
makes me feel, doubly so when I see your
hospitality to fellow believers.

—Philemon 1:7 MSG

*M*y first experience with cooking, apart from my
mother's supervision, was when my friend
Doris Fadney and I blew up a beaker of oatmeal in our high
school chemistry class. We poured the water and oatmeal
into a large beaker, set it over a flaming Bunsen burner, and
walked away to investigate the status of another project on
the opposite side of the room. After twenty minutes or so,
there was a loud explosion and we discovered that our oatmeal had not only coagulated but was now adhered to desks,
books, bottles of various chemicals, and other students as
well. Mr. Williamson, our teacher, showed a great deal of
consternation—and rightly so—but upon graduation, he
forgave us and we all had a good laugh.

Today, I love to cook, am crazy about new recipes, and am known to try add-ons when it comes to whipping up a soufflé, meatloaf, or casserole. It's all about the freedom to have fun and enjoy good fellowship. The great Austrian-born French chef, Wolfgang Puck, once said, "Cooking is my *kinderspiel*—child's play. You can make it yours, too. And while you're cooking, don't forget to share and laugh. Laugh a great deal, and with much love—it enhances the flavor of the food."[3]

A number of years ago, while visiting Marilyn Meberg and her family, she was working in the kitchen and I was sitting at the breakfast table, chatting and writing in a page of my journal. I had come to a spot that requested a favorite recipe, so I turned to Marilyn and asked, "Can you give me a recipe off the top of your head? Here's a page that calls for one," as I lifted the book and pointed to the square that needed to be filled in.

Without hesitation she said, "Sure." She spouted off this recipe I've saved for twenty years because it's so priceless.

Marilyn's Recipe for Smooth and Satiny Brown Gravy

4 C flour	2 tsp cinnamon
1 C arrowroot	1 tsp nutmeg
1 C fruit cocktail (with liquid)	1 Tbs salt
1 C raisins	Tbs white pepper

Take a 5 lb. rubber mallet; place in palm of right hand.

Methodically coerce lumps into satiny submission. Allow one hour for smooth and satiny effect. May be made ahead of time and stored for up to the return of Christ. Serve in silver, which enhances the flavor. Serves 23 guests, give or take 12.

Aunt Rebecca wanly commented after four bites: "Something's amiss . . ." Then she slipped into a coma.

Nothing could make me part with this recipe. I love it and remember the night I wrote it down.

Not only do I love recipes, but I'm a sucker for cookbooks. They're full of opportunities to express freedom and have fun. I counted mine not long ago—ninety-one. And I have favorites. They're the ones with brown spots and drops of whatever I was cooking and little burn marks on the side of the page. Some, yellowed with age, belonged to my grandmother and mother. They're among my treasures.

One of the most interesting is called *Manifold Destiny*, written by two guys: Chris Maynard and Bill Sheller.[4] It's all about cooking under the hood of your car. Their premise is that car-engine cooking brings people together and promotes sociability on the road. Can you believe it?

Not only does it include meals like "Hyundai Halibut with Fennel" (wrap in foil, place on engine, and drive approximately eighty-five miles), but it shows everything you need to know about your car while cooking a meal on it. (Originally the book cost $7.95, but I looked it up the other day on Amazon.com and it was selling for ninety-nine bucks.)

My favorite recipe in this cookbook is something called "To Grandmother's House Road Turkey." You slice a boneless turkey breast into thin strips and let it marinate in wine for about two hours. Then you take the turkey pieces and cover them with flour. Into five large buttered squares of foil you arrange equal amounts of turkey and veggies and pour heavy cream over that till it gets kind of soupy. Salt and pepper to taste, then seal each foil cup and tie it up. It takes about four hours to cook, so you need to drive at least 250 miles. Only once do you have to stop and turn the foil.

I've got recipes for everything—gourmet picnics, beach parties, children's festivities, wakes, weddings . . . the whole nine yards. In 1961, when I knew almost nothing about gourmet cooking, I decided to make a fancy little breakfast for a friend's birthday . . . to be served at midnight! Out of my Brennan's Restaurant cookbook from New Orleans, I chose the menu. The eight guests had no idea what they were getting into. Before it was over, everybody in the house was chopping shallots, mincing garlic, or stirring sauces. Amazingly, everything came out all right and *almost* on time. That whole group of friends is in glory now, but each time I pick up that cookbook, I remember my unforgettable party and those sweet companions of yesteryear.

Sometimes the most ordinary activities become opportunities to have fun when we feel free to express ourselves. We enjoy the process, connect with friends, and give ourselves the freedom to create memories that will ensure a feeling of joy and nostalgia many years down the road. Don't worry about getting everything right as much as having a good time. Consider camaraderie and conversation . . . conviviality and celebration . . . all the while creating memories with those you love!

And don't get hung up on the idea that you have to keep cooking the same old things over and over because you're afraid to be experimental. Be daring. Step out. Try new ideas. Have faith. You can't believe the fun you'll have. As Mark Twain said, "Eat what you like and let the food fight it out inside."

One of the finest chefs I know is Marilyn's son, Jeff Meberg. Cooking is not his "real" job, but it certainly could be. He's experimental, clever, and thoroughly enjoys being in the kitchen with freedom and fun as his cooking companions. I've known Jeff since he was seven, and together we've shared many creative adventures. One of the most enjoyable was on a cold January night when we decided to cook together, just the two of us. His wife, Carla, was visiting her parents in another state, so I invited him over and we made dinner. I always know I'll learn from Jeff and we'll have a million laughs. As Wolfgang Puck said, we enjoyed lots of *kinderspiel*.

We started with an appetizer of hot Brie with almonds on

crackers while deciding on a recipe from his *Paris Bistro* cookbook (which he brought with him), called "*Escallope de Saumon Frais Roti A'L'Huile D'Olive.*" In English that means "Fresh Salmon in a Sauce of Shallots, Tomatoes, Cream of Olive Oil." We served that with wild rice and green salad with Feta cheese. And for dessert we made Napoleons . . . served with fresh-ground Jamaican coffee.

I'll never forget that night. It was pouring down rain outside, lightning and thunder all around while we cooked up a storm. I had a roaring fire in my fireplace. We talked for hours and hours . . . about everything. At the end of the evening, Jeff wrote in my guestbook:

> Luci, the French salmon dish, with seedless, crushed tomatoes was great. An 8.5. It would have been a 10 if we'd only had crème fraîche . . . what a great time. Thank you so much for inviting me over when Carla is in Tulsa. Who would have guessed that almost twenty years ago, when I first met you, we would now get to share evenings together having *such* a wonderful time? Carla and I will always be there for you for the next twenty years! I love you a great deal. Next time it's crème fraîche and this pastry at my house! Love, Jeff Meberg

Have you ever read those lists when people name their ideal dinner guests? Often, the Lord's name is there. Have you noticed that? Do you wonder what the hostess would serve? Maybe it'd be catered, because home cooking wouldn't be nice enough for the Savior.

You know what I think? I don't think food would ever be the issue. The Lord isn't interested in that. He's interested in the spirit around the table, the joy that permeates conversation, and the freedom that makes everybody feel welcome. Amazingly, when all is said and done, mealtime isn't about the food; it's about the guests, the fellowship, and the love they share . . . the fun they have. We need to remember that!

In Martha Stewart's new cookbook, she includes a recipe for "Oatmeal and Whole Wheat Waffles with Mango Sauce and Fresh Fruit." Maybe I'd serve that if Jesus came to eat at my house. Since I've never made it, why not? If I can locate Doris Fadney, that'd be a fun meal to make together. We're good with oatmeal.

God, I don't thank you often enough for my family
and friends. Thank you for the love we share and for
the fun we have together.

Freedom to Hold Hands with Heaven

Sheila Walsh

> Andrew, Simon Peter's brother, spoke up, "Here is a
> boy with five small barley loaves and two small fish,
> but how far will they go among so many?"
>
> —John 6:8–9 NIV

*B*en, did you eat your lunch?"

It was the same question every day. He prepared his answer on the walk home from school with his best friend, Luke. Ben and Luke would kick the dusty road with their sandals until clouds formed over their heads, and they would cough and laugh and laugh and cough. Then Ben would rehearse, "Yes, Mom, I ate my lunch. No, Mom, I'm not kidding. Yes, Mom, every bite . . . and it was deeeelicious!"

When he got home, he knew his mom would laugh at that and make a poor attempt at swatting him with a towel.

It was a mystery to Ben and Luke why mothers were so obsessed with food. "What I can't understand," Luke said, "is why my mom is always trying to stuff anything that's not moving into my mouth when she hardly eats enough herself to keep a frog alive. I guess it's because Dad says her figure gets more like an orange every day!"

They laughed at that thought as they parted for the day, Ben to one side of the hill, Luke to the other. "See you tomorrow, Ben," Luke called over his shoulder. "Remember, my mom invited you over to play after school."

"I remember. Bye!"

When he got home, Ben knocked his shoes on the side of the house to shake off most of the sandy dust. "Mom, I'm home!" he called as he went inside. "And I ate my lunch, in case you were wondering!"

Ben was a picky eater and small for his age, so Elizabeth, like all good mothers, worried about his health. "Well, I'm glad to hear it," she said with a smile as she swatted him with a towel.

The next morning as the sun streamed through the kitchen, Elizabeth called, "Ben! Are you up yet?"

"Yeah, I'm up," he called back.

"Are you actually out of bed with both feet on the floor?" she asked.

How do mothers know that stuff? Ben wondered as he forced his right foot to join his left foot on the floor.

"I packed you something special for lunch today," his mom said as Ben dragged his sleepy form into the kitchen. "It's one of your favorites: a couple of pickled fish and a few fresh-baked rolls, hot out of the oven."

"What's a few, Mom?" Ben asked. "Enough to feed the whole school?"

"That's enough of that, young man. I'll be checking your lunch box when you get home!"

"Okay. I'll be in a little later today, Mom, remember? Luke's mom invited me over to play for a while."

"That's fine. Just remember your manners and be home before dinner."

As the afternoon shadows began to grow long over Luke's house later that day, Luke's mom said, "It's getting late, Ben. I think you should head home now. Don't forget your lunch box."

Lunch box! Ben thought. *Oh no, I forgot to eat my lunch! Well, maybe I'll meet a hungry dog on the way home.*

Ben wandered down the lane and headed toward the hill between his house and Luke's. It was usually deserted at this time of afternoon, but today there was a huge crowd ahead of him. Ben had never seen so many people. *What's going on?* he wondered.

He tried to see, but the crowd was too thick. He got down on his hands and knees and made his way through a maze of legs and robes and sandals until he got to the front, where a man was talking.

Ben didn't recognize him, but his voice was like a waterfall, soothing and fresh. After a few moments, the man stopped. Some of his friends were whispering in his ear. Ben watched their worried expressions. They seemed very cross.

Am I going to get in trouble for pushing to the front? he thought, as one of the men came toward the crowd. Then Ben heard the man ask if anyone had any food.

This is better than giving my lunch to a dog, Ben thought as he stood up to offer his slightly battered lunch. The man didn't seem entirely thrilled with Ben's meager offering, but he took it anyway and gave it to the man who didn't seem worried at all. Ben watched this man named Jesus lift Ben's little lunch up to the sky.

What's he doing with it? Ben wondered, wide-eyed. The crowd became very quiet, as if they were all wondering the same thing.

"Taking the five loaves and the two fish and looking up to heaven, he gave thanks and broke the loaves. Then he gave them to his disciples to set before the people. He also divided the two fish among them all" (Mark 6:41 NIV).

Ben could not believe his eyes! He knew what he had in his lunch box. He had five of his mom's little rolls and two little pickled fish. But as he watched, this Jesus kept dividing it and dividing it, and there was more and more and more. Jesus' friends began distributing the food to the crowd. Ben looked at the man beside him. That one man seemed to have in his hand more bread and fish than Ben had in his lunch box to begin with! Everyone was eating as much as they wanted.

Ben had some of the food, too, and it tasted better than anything he could remember from his mom's kitchen. When it was all over and the people began to go home, Ben watched as some of the men who were with Jesus gathered up baskets full of what was left over. There was enough to feed Ben's whole school for a week!

Wait till I tell Luke about this! Ben thought. *He'll never believe it.*

Ben hurried home, realizing that he was much later than he had told his mother he would be. He ran into the house. "Mom, Mom! Where are you?"

"Where am *I*?" his mom said as she came out of the bedroom. "Where have *you* been, young man? Do you know what time it is? I was just about to walk over to Luke's house and fetch you back myself."

"But Mom . . . have I got something to tell you!"

That's all we know of this boy's story. He gave what he had to Jesus, and in return he got to see what God can do when heaven and earth hold hands. This miracle on a hillside is repeated over and over every day from Pittsburgh to Paris, from New York to New Zealand. It is the mystery and miracle that everyone who believes in Jesus Christ is invited to participate in—bring all you have to the table, and see what God will do!

I see it every weekend at Women of Faith conferences across America. I stand at the back of the arena every Friday night and watch as fifteen to twenty thousand women take their seats. Some are in the best days of their lives, and some are in the worst. Some come with friends, while others wander in alone. But all gather there for the same reason. Every one wants to be fed by Jesus, whether they know it or not.

As a team, we gather to pray before each conference. As we look at what we have to offer to this vast crowd, it is clear to us that all we have is bread and fish for a few. So we take our little lunch, and we bring it to Jesus—and then something miraculous happens. He takes it and blesses it and feeds his people.

Too often we miss the point as daughters of the King. We look at what we have to offer, and it is clear to us that it's not enough so we hold back. Yet the fact that we don't have enough is the whole point. We are given the outrageous invitation to partner with the King of kings as he lavishes his love and grace on this earth. God uses little boys' lunches and women's conferences and a few words spoken in kindness—and through these simple vessels, he changes the world.

Whatever you have today is enough. It might not look like it to you, but put into Jesus's hands, it is more than enough.

———

Father God, today I bring my life to you as an offering. I ask that you would do what only you can do as I slip my hand into yours and watch as heaven touches earth.

Freedom to Be Generous

Nicole Johnson

So let each one give as he purposes in his heart,
not grudgingly or of necessity; for God
loves a cheerful giver.

—2 Corinthians 9:7 NKJV

I heard their laughter in the hallway first. The door opened, and three young, professional women walked through the door of the day spa where I was getting a quick manicure. I couldn't see them right away, but they came into my sightline as one of them, I'll call her Bonnie, approached the reception desk. They were all carrying briefcases and were apparently there for some sort of business appointment. Bonnie asked to speak to someone, and then Bonnie and her friends stood around chatting and waiting for the person they had requested. But when a woman came out with a white terrycloth robe and slippers for Bonnie and took her briefcase and handbag in exchange, Bonnie's two friends started laughing and clapping.

Needless to say, I was terribly curious. I can smell a celebration, even through nail polish remover, and I was dying to know what was going on.

They were there for another fifteen minutes or so, and then the two friends departed and Bonnie was taken into the spa. After the commotion subsided, I asked the receptionist what had happened. She said that the friends had booked their coworker, Bonnie, for a day at the spa as a surprise. They had set up a "day of meetings" and were coming to their first "appointment" to meet with the director of the spa, who happened to be a real client of the firm that all three women worked for. When the woman came out to see them carrying the robe and slippers, it was then that Bonnie's friends informed her they had cleared her calendar, and the "day of meetings" had been replaced by scheduled spa treatments, including a facial and massage. They all hugged and then instructed Bonnie to have fun and they would be back to pick her up at four thirty.

What a great idea by great friends! What a thoughtful gift. The thing I love the most about this kind of creative caring is that it is generous in every way I can think of—in heart, in spirit, in money, and in time. I'm smiling as I remember it now.

The receptionist was smiling, too, as she recounted to me what had happened. As she returned to the front desk, she joked, "I think I need new friends!" We both laughed. When things were quiet again, I found myself grateful for my own generous friends who have made my life so rich with their love and care.

A generous person is free. Really free—way down deep on the inside. She is free to live with open hands, sharing all she has as she walks through life. Generosity frees a person to hold all material things loosely. Not just so she can give what she has away, but so that nothing has a hold or a tight grip on her heart or mind. A tight grip of money on the heart makes the hands grip tightly on the wallet, but a generous person is free to hold her wallet loosely because her heart is free.

A generous person knows the deep joy found in giving to others, but she is also able to receive when given to. Because she knows the joy given to the generous, she would never want to deprive others of that joy by not allowing them to give. It is wonderful fun to watch two generous people argue over who gets to pay the check after dinner. The focus is not who is going to pay the bill; it is about who is going to rob the other one of the joy of picking up the tab for a special evening. Generosity is a beautiful quality.

Interestingly enough, it is never money or any kind of physical abundance that makes a person generous. It would seem that the more you have, the more you might be willing to share or give away—but sadly, that just isn't true. Some of the most generous people I've known have little in their bank accounts but give significantly to those in need. And then there are millionaires who refuse to use their resources to help anyone but themselves. A person with monetary wealth can be dirt-poor in her heart. No, the only abundance that must be present in the life of a generous person is the abundance of the heart and spirit. It is this abundance that sets the heart and mind free, and the wallet simply follows.

The generosity that lives and grows inside a person usually starts with gratitude for whatever she has, much or little. I could tell that Bonnie's friends were grateful women—I don't have to know them or even know their names to know this. It was demonstrated so clearly in their actions. They *saw* Bonnie, as well as her hard work, and they wanted to do something for her. People don't *see* other people when they are only focused on themselves. They don't think about how they might lighten someone else's load if they are always looking for someone to carry part of theirs. People are not generous if they are ungrateful in their hearts for what they have.

And then came my second thought about this incident with Bonnie. The receptionist and I had been thinking about our own friends in light of what Bonnie's friends had done for her. But I found myself considering this: more than *having* friends like that, how can I *be* a friend like that? Bonnie's friends personified generosity. They demonstrated (right before my very eyes) the amazing freedom of their hearts with that generous and gracious act of friendship.

I want to be more like Bonnie's friends. It's not that I'm stingy or miserly—no, that would be pretty easy to recognize in myself—I'm just busy and too often thoughtless because of my preoccupation with other things. I'm often trapped by the manyness and muchness of life. I don't always take the time to *see* the others around me or ask myself how I can make their lives better and richer. I've talked myself out of generosity before, settling more comfortably for what seemed sensible and practical.

But God is never this way. His love is not sensible and practical; it is lavish and extravagant, and it sets us free to be generous with those around us. We can know in our hearts the kind of abundance that will release our white-knuckled hold on our possessions or even on our time. And then we are free to be as generous as Bonnie's wonderful friends.

Gracious God, thank you for lavishing gifts of love and mercy upon us. May we receive these abundant gifts and be free to lavish them upon others. Teach us how to open our hearts that we might open our hands in generosity to those around us.

Freedom to *Bee* Still

Thelma Wells

Be still, and know that I am God;
I will be exalted among the nations,
I will be exalted in the earth!

—Psalm 46:10 NKJV

*H*ave you ever noticed how much noise is going on around you? I didn't either, until several people called my attention to the amount of noise in my home. In my living room, I have an old grandfather clock that sounds off in grand style every thirty minutes as if it were Big Ben. In my office, a clock on the wall with angels painted on each hour has the same, less noisy sound, but the time is set just a little off from the grandfather clock. In my sunroom, another wall clock with revolving crystal angels plays the same tune a bit more somber. I use my cell phone as an alarm clock to wake me in the mornings and to remind me of deadlines during the day, and the volume is up as high as it can go.

Beside the clocks sounding off, my intercom (which reaches every area in my house) softly plays praise music twenty-four hours a day, along with the CD player in my bedroom, one softly playing in my office, and the computer music playing just loud enough for me to hear it from Pat and Karole's office (along with their contagious laughter when something's funny). Add all that to the television on in the den when my husband's at home and the other one playing in another bedroom when my grandchildren are there.

When I'm cooking, I set the timer on the oven so I won't burn down the house. Not to mention the constant ringing of the four-line business phone, the four house phones, and the several cell phones playing different musical renditions that get our attention all day long.

Because I have one office in my house where I and two other ladies work, we have the fax machine, the copy machine, the printers, and the postage meter accelerating the noise factor. Plus, I have an alarm set on each of my five entry doors to let me know when people are entering or leaving my home.

Its *dong, dong, dong, dong . . . dong, dong, dong, dong*—or *ring, ring*—or *tick, tick*—or music or laughter or talk or tinkling or buzzer amid the swish of the oscillating ceiling fans all day long.

With all this going on at the same time, it's no wonder people get confused when my doorbell rings, also sounding like a loud Big Ben. People ask, "Is that the doorbell or the clock?" I can always tell the difference, depending on the noise level.

I was reminded of all the noise in my house while sitting in a hotel room and listening to all the sounds around me. There was the traffic driving on the highway that runs parallel to the hotel window, the sound of doors opening and shutting, the tinkle of the breakfast trays rattling down the hall, water running in the bathroom as people showered for the day, cell phones ringing, sirens blasting, the echo of someone's voice over the cell phone, and even my little friendly reminder on my computer telling me, "You've got mail!"

Our minds are so covered with the external noises of everyday life and the internal noises of our thoughts and self-talk that it's often difficult to hear the voice of God speaking to us. What would happen if we stopped all the Big Bens and televisions, radios, CDs, and DVDs and closed our ears to our busy thoughts and self-talk?

I've done that twice this year. I stopped those noises by going to a secluded place where the only noise was the occasional sound of the wind and chirp of a bird. I got facedown on the floor and offered myself to God while I talked to him and, more importantly, where he could talk to me. It's amazing how he doesn't use a lot of words; he just speaks peace and contentment in our hearts. When he speaks words to my heart, they are usually very simple like, *Trust me! Wait on me. I love you with an everlasting love. Cast your cares on me. I will provide for you. I am your Shield and Buckle. I will rejoice over you with singing. I will take care of your children. I will heal your heart. You are mine, and I will protect you.*

It's amazing how we can get so caught up with other noises, voices, interruptions, irritations, and agitations from the world around us that we fail to remember that the only voice that can give us pure wisdom, unmarred guidance, peace we can't understand, hope that will not disappoint, strength to make it through our problems, contentment instead of confusion, and patience to stand when all around us is falling is the still, small, sovereign voice of God.

It's difficult to shut your mind to the internal noises that we struggle with daily. We don't even have to name them, do we? You know what I mean: finances, relationships, goals, dreams, worries, cares, concerns, emotions, and the list goes on. Sometimes these internal thoughts are actually louder than the noises we hear externally. But I've found that I need a quiet position and place to rest these internal distractions and focus on God.

I find that lying facedown on the floor and picturing Jesus (as I see him) and speaking directly to him refocuses my attention from the outside things of this world to the only Person who matters. Often when I get on my knees, I put my hands over my eyes and concentrate on him. In the bathtub, I am surrounded with clean aromatic smells and foaming white bubbles, taking me to a place of relaxation so I can meditate on him. Some of the most poignant messages I have received from God have come when I am relaxed and focusing on him.

None of this concentration and meditation can be done without invoking the presence of the Holy Spirit and meditating on the words God has given us in the Bible. After all, the Spirit is our earthly advocate to the Father in prayer (John 14:26) and the Bible is God's Living Word to us. Jesus is sitting at God's right hand in heaven, and he "always lives to make intercession" for us (Hebrews 7:25 NKJV). Just think! We have the Holy Spirit and the Savior praying for us when we are in the holy place of prayer with our Lord.

To be still requires not only focusing on God and his Word but also relying on him to do what he says. If you've not been in a place of quiet and consecrated communion with the Lord where noise is not a distraction, try it. You'll be amazed at what God will speak to you. He longs to communicate with you and give you peace.

Whether on the floor, on my knees, or in the bathtub, I pause in a position of intimacy with God. My love for him, my pursuit of him through his Word, my praise of him, and my worship of him delivers me to a place of intimacy with him so that he and I can freely communicate with each other. I have the amazing freedom to get close to God, to talk to God, and to believe with all my being that he is there to hear me and help me.

I suggest that today—as soon as possible—you exercise your freedom in Christ to be still. Get quiet, get in position, get focused, and then get ready for one of the greatest experiences of your life: communication with the God of everything, who knows and sees everything and who wants to tell you something!

Here I am, Lord. For the next few minutes, I will turn off or ignore the noise and daily distractions of my life so I can be still and quiet, ready to hear from you!

Freedom to Serve
One Another

Luci Swindoll

Serve one another in love.

—Galatians 5:13 NIV

*G*rowing up in my family was a microcosm of how I live today. My mother and dad were always around, helping us kids with homework, listening to our problems, breaking up squabbles, encouraging us to do the best we could, laughing at our antics, and dealing with our individual eccentricities and concerns. They modeled Christ in their lives and held him in high esteem when it came to their primary allegiance. It was very common to see my mother praying, reading her Bible, or asking us questions that had to do with a meaningful, rich life.

Not only did my parents display lives that were centered in Christ, but they were balanced in their interests. They loved sports, games, picnics, and gatherings of all kinds.

They read the daily newspaper and books and often talked about what they learned from the printed page. They delighted in having dinner parties, inviting everyone in the neighborhood. They helped out when others were sick or grieving or lonely. They loved surprises and often showed up with a big pot of coffee or homemade cookies for a family who just moved into the neighborhood. They even loaned money to folks who were down on their luck. In short, our family was a very active little community.

Oh, and I almost forgot . . . the craziness. We all had so much fun! Starting with my grandmother, who lived about forty-five minutes away and came to see us often with nutty stories to tell and family jokes to share. Or when we went to see her, we acted out in her living room our homespun plays with costumes, makeup, and lots of corny one-upmanship. All in all, the entire collective clan was an off-Broadway show just waiting to be discovered.

I want to also mention that my family was not without our pains, hurts, disappointments, and feelings of being overlooked or left out. We certainly had many opportunities to talk to the Lord about being upset with a parent or a sibling who didn't do what we wanted or said something that hurt us. In other words, we were all very much in the human condition when it came to good and bad, happiness and sorrow, understanding and lack of it.

That picture of the past is a snapshot of my present circumstances in so many ways. I live in a neighborhood with friends from thirty years ago, pals from Women of Faith, family, and lots of neighbors whom I'm getting to know a little better each day. With the exception of Thelma, the entire Women of Faith speaking team lives within walking distance of each other in Frisco, Texas, just north of Dallas. And Thelma is only a twenty-minute drive south. Everybody is bonded together in one way or another. We shop at the same grocery store, have the same handyman, rely on the same gardener, make appointments with the same doctor, call on the same cleaning lady, use the same pest-control guy, go to the same church, and eat at the same restaurants. We see each other all the time. We throw parties, go to meetings, take care of each other when we're sick and tired, and put on our own little theater antics. We laugh and sing and pray and cry and work together. Why do we do this? What makes us live this way? Why are we so close and share the same community? Because we love each other.

We believe God has given us this bond of oneness as a gift from him. This close-knit community sets us free from fear and releases us from the concerns of growing old alone. It also gives us freedom to enjoy a place of rich fellowship and oneness of spirit. I can't imagine living anywhere else.

Recently, I read an article in the Davis, California, newspaper about a group of twelve friends (average age of eighty) who got together to pioneer a new kind of commune. (Granted, we're not as old as they . . . but we're getting there.) They decided they wanted to face their senior years on their own terms, so they planned and executed a small housing development for themselves and their friends called "Glacier Circle." Over the past five years, these residents found and bought land together, hired an architect together, figured out the needed insurance together, lobbied for zoning changes together, and moved into the same neighborhood together. A seventy-nine-year-old family therapist in the group said, "We recognized that when you're physically closer to each other, you pay more attention, look in on each other. The idea is to share care." There are four couples, two widows, and two who live alone—and all together they make a community that knows the needs of each other and helps in every way they can to make life easier, richer, sweeter, and more fun.

A few months ago when Ney Bailey, one of our friends around the corner and down the street, got very sick and needed immediate attention, I picked her up from her home and took her to an emergency-care facility about a mile away. When I arrived, my cell phone was ringing with a call from Barry Walsh (Sheila's husband) asking if he could come and sit with me. Of course! In a while, Mary came with Patsy. We prayed for Ney and for the doctor taking care of her. When we finally got permission, we all went to her examination room and stayed with her until she was able to leave.

One person took her home, another went for her medications, and a third went to her house to get her bed ready for arrival. It was clockwork, and nobody felt the burden of having to do it all. We "shared the care." And not only that, but when we tucked her in bed that night, we raided her refrigerator and sat around the kitchen table talking and praying for hours.

There are also the nutty, fun times like last summer, when Sheila's son, Christian, graduated from the second grade. His parents gave him a little party at one of our favorite haunts in Frisco, the Double Dip. It's a drive-through restaurant with the best ice cream this side of the Mississippi. We took our pets, ordered double-dip cones, and sat outside on benches, laughing and talking as we watched the sun set in the distance. We asked Christian about his school days and congratulated him on the awards he'd won at the end of the year. It was great fun! Very soon he'll be graduating again, and we'll enjoy a repeat performance.

Who doesn't want to live in a neighborhood like that?

In Galatians 5:13, the apostle Paul says, "Serve one another in love" (NIV). He encourages us to use our freedom in love, serving one another because that's how freedom grows. If we love others as we love ourselves, that's an act of true freedom, he says. It doesn't matter the age of the person or whether or not they make the same salary as we do. It matters that we live freely to serve one another. When this happens, there's a willingness to be involved in loyal commitment toward each other and a desire to make life easier for those we love.

At the Hartford, Connecticut, Women of Faith conference last year, a woman came to my table and handed me a card that read, "Until you are willing to be a servant, you will always be a slave to something." I've thought of that a million times and every day find it to be truer.

Paul continues in Galatians 5:16–18:

> My counsel is this: Live freely, animated and motivated by God's Spirit. Then you won't feed the compulsions of selfishness. For there is a root of sinful self-interest in us that is at odds with a free spirit, just as the free spirit is incompatible with selfishness. These two ways of life are antithetical, so that you cannot live at times one way and at times another way according to how you feel on any given day. Why don't you choose to be led by the Spirit and to escape the erratic compulsions of a law-dominated existence? (MSG)

Life will always have its imperfections, and neighborhoods will always have their challenges. But we've been made to rise above those concerns by the power of God's Spirit. As Paul says in his closing sentence in Galatians 5: "We have far more interesting things to do with our lives. Each of us is an original" (v. 26 MSG).

Look around and see how you can serve others. Enter into their lives with a servant spirit. Think of fun things to do for the kids and caring ways to help lift a neighbor's load. Laugh, sing, and dance until your voice and knees give out. You have no idea how much fun it will be and how rich your life will become.

———

God, show me how I can serve a friend or neighbor today.
May I enjoy the freedom that comes by loving others
as I love myself.

Freedom to Give

Mary Graham

Give, and it will be given to you: good measure, pressed down, shaken together, and running over will be put into your bosom. For with the same measure that you use, it will be measured back to you.

—Luke 6:38 NKJV

My mother modeled giving, even though we had a very large family (I'm the youngest of eight siblings) and her resources were very limited. Quite frankly, I don't ever remember having enough of anything. We were short on rooms in the house, money in the bank, clothes on our backs, and food on the table. Nonetheless, no one ever spoke of what we lacked.

My mother also set a very high standard of generosity. It was always okay for us to invite someone to stay overnight at our house, and my mother never required us to get prior permission. It was always fine to include a friend at mealtime. I'm sure there was never enough time in my mother's day to get everything done she needed to do (we had no modern conveniences, including plumbing, most of my life), yet I watched her set aside occasions for her friends when they dropped by needing her time or attention.

We didn't have food to spare as far as I could tell, but when someone died, my mother went straight to the kitchen and made something to take the family. When the schoolteachers asked for cakes for the cake walk, cookies for the bake sale, or someone to make uniforms for the primary band, all eight of us felt very free to volunteer our mother and she never once let us down. One night she made four angel food cakes because three brothers and I, each in a separate homeroom, had volunteered a cake. My mother never flinched.

And although our resources were exceedingly limited, we knew we could share anything we had. One of my brother's friends in high school wasn't getting along with his parents, so my brother told him he could live with us—which he did, for four months. She gave from a generous heart, and for whatever reason, she never ran out. She had the freedom to give, and in so doing, she modeled giving for us. And our family always had enough, even though for many years my father was without work and my mother wrote a newspaper column for only seventeen dollars a week.

It's one of the great legacies left to us by our wonderful mother. Everyone in my family is generous of heart and spirit. Many examples come to mind of how my family members have given of themselves to others in a thousand ways.

I was born the day after one of my sisters became a teenager. She's told me all my life that Mother gave me to her as her birthday present. All her life, this sister took a special interest in me and tried to ensure that I would never need or want for anything. I was only four when she left for college, but she never forgot me. She made sure I had everything I needed and almost everything I ever wanted.

As a teenager, I spent summers being the nanny for her three little boys. When I graduated from high school, she made sure I had money for college. Whenever I met anyone in those years who needed a home and a surrogate mother, I took them to my sister's house. When I decided to go into Christian ministry, she helped make sure I had full financial support. After being in the ministry a few years, she bought a house where I could live. She believed I needed a place to practice hospitality and reach out to others. That house became known as the "party" house. It was dubbed that by the child of a friend of ours who often asked to go there, assuming we were always having a party in the same way she assumed McDonald's was always serving hamburgers.

The first year I lived there, we hosted more than 350 guests for a meal or to spend the night. (I only know that because Luci Swindoll once counted the names in the guest book!) We had fifteen people for lunch the day we moved in. I had no furniture yet, but there were plenty of places to sit on the floor. It was wonderful having a place people loved and feeling the freedom to use it.

Actually, all my sisters are like her. They didn't all have the capacity for giving that my older sister had, but they were all giving. Their homes have always been a refuge for others and their kitchens always bustling with activity, people of all ages, and the scent of something wonderful in the oven. Through the years, I've taken literally hundreds of guests to the homes of my sisters. I never asked if it was okay because I knew it was. It was the way we lived. We caught it from our mother.

What I loved about my mother, I love about God. God gives and gives and gives. "He gave His only begotten Son, that whoever believes in Him should not perish but have everlasting life" (John 3:16 NKJV). And, "He who did not spare His own Son, but delivered Him up for us all, how shall He not with Him also freely give us all things?" (Romans 8:32 NKJV). And he gives us each day "our daily bread" (Matthew 6:11 NKJV). He gives wisdom "liberally" to anyone who asks (James 1:5 NKJV). And my favorite: "He gives more grace. Therefore He says, 'God resists the proud, but gives grace to the humble'" (James 4:6 NKJV).

Our God is exceedingly generous, and believe it or not, that quality is contagious. My mother got it from him and passed it along to us.

I have to say, however, one word of caution about this. Occasionally, I've personally been a little too free with my giving. I've been known to give away objects owned by my friends without even thinking. ("But Ney, she really wanted it and I thought you wouldn't mind!") I've given promises I couldn't keep. ("Of course you can stay at Luci's house. She won't mind at all!") And I've given someone else's time when it was not mine to give. ("I'm sure Marilyn will be happy to speak at your son's school.") I try to remember (although it doesn't always work for me) that I can only give away what is *mine.* In that, freedom has its limitations.

A friend of mine has the gift of giving. She mostly gives money, but the amount she gives astounds me and those to whom it is given. She tithes 25 percent of her gross income to the cause of Christ here and around the world. She is single and was at one time afraid to tithe at all. A family member challenged her, so she started with 11 percent. She found her income increased, so she increased her tithe. She's still giving more and more every year because as she says, "I keep having more and more to give." On top of her tithe, she gives in the sweetest and most charitable ways—sometimes to groups she believes in and sometimes to individuals in need. I've known her to buy kitchen appliances, computers, and automobiles for people, just because she becomes aware of the need. In her heart, she feels free to give so she gives freely. When I watch her, I want to give more.

She tells me that the thing that used to keep her from giving was that she was afraid she'd run out. That's a terrifying thought, and anyone can understand feeling limited in their giving if that was their perspective. But in Luke 6:38, Jesus says, "Give, and it will be given to you: good measure, pressed down, shaken together, and running over will be put into your bosom. For with the same measure that you use, it will be measured back to you" (NKJV). I read that and believe that the more freely we give, the more freely we receive. I believe it not only because I read it but because I've seen it demonstrated again and again in the lives of my family and friends.

Interestingly, I have often seen this principle at work in the lives of people who have little more than in those who have much. If you wait for more space, more money, more time, or more riches before you commit to give, you're likely to wait forever.

I'm so grateful my mother didn't wait to give—nor did my sisters, nor have most of my friends. Seeing the freedom with which they give of themselves and their time and their money, the more I learn to be like them in the ways they are free to be like Jesus.

Lord, help me to become more generous in heart and spirit. Show me today how I can give to others—my time or my money or myself—so I can be more like you.

Freedom to Sit at His Feet

Sheila Walsh

While Jesus and his followers were traveling, Jesus went
into a town. A woman named Martha let Jesus stay at her
house. Martha had a sister named Mary, who was sitting
at Jesus' feet and listening to him teach. But Martha was
busy with all the work to be done. She went in and said,
"Lord, don't you care that my sister has left me alone
to do all the work? Tell her to help me."
But the Lord answered her, "Martha, Martha, you are
worried and upset about many things. Only one thing
is important. Mary has chosen the better thing, and
it will never be taken away from her."

—Luke 10:38–42 NCV

She had such a lot to do today. The house needed to
be swept, there was laundry to be done, and she had-
n't even begun to think about the evening meal.

"Where does time go?" she asked herself as she hurried
through the marketplace. It was unusually busy today. People
pushed and bumped up against one another. Two boys were
playing tag in the crowd, and one stepped on her foot and
made her drop her bag of pomegranates.

"Watch where you are going, young man!" she cried, but the dark-haired boy was already lost in the crowd.

"Mary, help me pick these up before they are ruined," she said to her sister. "I don't know what is wrong with young people these days. They seem to have no respect for their elders!"

Mary smiled. "Oh, Martha, they're just being boys. Don't you remember when Lazarus was a boy and he ran through the house with his friend Isaac and knocked over Mom's entire meal?"

"I do indeed," Martha replied. "Mother worked on preparing that meal all day. What thanks did she get?"

"Well . . . the neighborhood dogs seemed grateful," Mary replied with a smile. "Look, Martha, just ahead—isn't that Peter?"

The two sisters greeted their friend and were thrilled when Peter told them that Jesus was back in town and that he would love to stay with them that evening.

"You must all come for a meal!" Martha offered, already going over the menu in her mind. She knew that Jesus must be tired from all his travels, and she would make sure that tonight he would eat well and rest.

"Let's hurry, Mary," she said. "There's a lot to be done."

Hurrying was the last thing on Mary's mind. All she wanted to do was to sit at Jesus' feet. That evening as Jesus taught, Mary sat and listened. She drank in every word.

Every now and then, they would hear a loud clang from the kitchen, a dropped pan or plate. Martha hurried in and out, bringing more food, making sure everyone had enough to drink. She tried to get her sister's attention, but Mary was caught up in every word that Jesus spoke.

Finally, Martha had had enough. No one seemed to notice that this was a two-woman household but only one woman was doing all the work. She was surprised that Jesus hadn't said anything to Mary, so she said to him, "Lord, don't you care that my sister has left me alone to do all the work? Tell her to help me."

There was a moment of awkward silence as every head turned to look at Martha's flustered and flushed complexion. In that moment, Mary was transported back through the years. She was five years old, and Martha was saying to their mother, "Mom, Mary's staring out the window again. Tell her to help me with the chores!"

Then Jesus spoke, and Mary was back in the moment. His voice was full of love and tenderness as he looked into Martha's eyes and said, "Martha, Martha, you are worried and upset about many things. Only one thing is important. Mary has chosen the better thing, and it will never be taken away from her" (Luke 10:41–42 NCV).

Martha's eyes filled with tears. If Jesus had only said her name once, it would have bruised her—but he said it twice, as if speaking to a child. Mary reached her hand out and took her sister's rougher hand in hers. So much was said with so few words.

More than any other woman in the New Testament, Mary of Bethany had chosen her place at the feet of Jesus. The Gospels record three separate occasions when Mary is found there. She sat at his feet to learn, she fell at his feet to weep, and she bent over his feet to anoint him for what lay ahead. The body language of the two sisters is revealing.

When Martha addressed Jesus in her home, he would have been reclining. It would be fairly safe to assume that Martha either bent over to address him or stood over him, while Mary took the lowest place at his feet.

When their brother, Lazarus, died and Jesus finally made his way to Bethany, Martha ran out to see him and confronted him on the road. She said, "Lord, if you had been here, my brother would not have died" (John 11:21 NCV). Mary stayed in the house until Jesus asked for her. Then we read that she came out and fell at his feet. John's Gospel tells that Mary said exactly the same thing as Martha had said, but from a very different place (v. 32). She said it from a place of humility and tears, once again at Jesus' feet.

The third occasion took place six days before Passover. Mary and Martha were hosting a meal in their home in Jesus' honor. Mary took a jar of expensive perfume and anointed his feet. She seems at this point in the narrative to be the one most sensitive to the approaching sacrificial death of Christ.

The perfume she used would have cost what an average worker would make in a year. Her offering deeply touched the heart of Christ. She poured a pint of pure nard over his weary feet and dried the excess with her hair.

Many good books and articles have been written about the differences between Mary and Martha, about how we can have Mary's heart in a world that flies past at Martha's pace. For me, the lesson I take from Mary is a simple one. If you or I had been invited to have coffee with Mary and Martha on the morning after Jesus ate at their home, it might have been interesting to ask them some questions like these:

"What was the most important thing Jesus said last night?"

"What did he say that you have carried with you into this new day?"

"What do you understand now that you didn't understand yesterday morning?"

If you asked them both, "Do you love Jesus?" I am convinced that Mary and Martha would both have said yes. The discrepancy might appear in what they had taken from that day into the next one. Long after Jesus' death and resurrection, Mary must have treasured every word that she learned at his feet. When difficult days came and persecution began to visit the church, Mary had a treasure chest of internal strength to draw upon because of what she learned on her knees at the feet of Christ.

I don't know what your schedule is like today. I don't

know how long your to-do list is or how many people have expectations of you. If you are anything like me, I often find myself at the end of another day and wonder where all the hours went and how much I really accomplished. I love the fact that Martha wanted to take care of Jesus and serve him and his friends. I'm sure her practical offerings and hospitality gave him many moments of respite in a very tiring schedule. But I want to learn what it looks like, today, to sit at Jesus's feet. Our world is changing at such a rapid pace. We don't know what today or tomorrow will hold, but Jesus does.

Christ's death and sacrifice bought us freedom from condemnation and promises peace and joy for our journey. I don't want my freedom to disintegrate into being free to run around doing things all the time; rather, I want to treasure my freedom to sit at his feet and learn. I want to sit at his feet and worship. I choose to sit at his feet and pour my life out as an offering to him.

God, no matter how busy my life is today, I choose
to sit at your feet and worship you.

Freedom to Get Our Affairs in Order

Nicole Johnson

> The sting of death is sin, and the strength of sin
> is the law. But thanks be to God, who gives us
> the victory through our Lord Jesus Christ.
>
> —1 Corinthians 15:56–57 NKJV

*D*eath is not an easy subject. A reader wouldn't expect to find a devotional on death in a book on freedom. Unless you start thinking about being free from your body of pain or how belief in a glorious heaven affects your life on earth—then it fits perfectly. But that's not what I intend to write about.

As a follower of Christ, who taught his disciples that this world is as bad as it gets for those who believe in him, I find myself free to make plans regarding my death. He told those closest to him, "I go to prepare a place for you" (John 14:2 NKJV). That is a great promise in Scripture, and I don't mind thinking ahead about changing addresses one day and moving there. Don't get me wrong; it's not easy to think about suffering, nor is it easy to think about dying. But in faith, we hold to the same assurance as the apostle Paul, who said, "O death, where is your victory? O death, where is your sting?" (1 Corinthians 15:55 NLT).

If death is not victorious, then we have a lot to be thankful for amid the sadness of someone's passing. We have incredible freedom to trust that suffering has ended and something wonderful has begun, despite the ache in our hearts over what we personally have lost.

I have been working on my last will and testament for at least two years. This is a conservative estimate because the truth is, I've lost track of the time. It wasn't something I wanted to do when I started it, but I was convinced it needed to be done. I'm not generally a procrastinator, but I will admit there is never an opportune moment to work on one's will, so it's very easy to put off. I believe this must be true for almost everyone. It seems such an unpleasant subject that we delay starting and then never get around to it—even though we know we should.

Last year, after a completely unexpected and tragic loss in our family, I could clearly see the value of doing this hard work. Actually, I could see the devastating consequences of not having done it. No one can explain this better than someone on whose shoulders it falls not only to sort out someone's estate but to make the personal decisions around a loved one's death. This sad and difficult loss removed the blanket of silence surrounding getting one's affairs in order and has caused me to become more zealous about this subject with those I care about.

When we put our trust in God, we put our trust in his promise of eternal life and a glorious heaven. This brings wonderful freedom, whether it completely eliminates the fear of death or not. This allows us to take responsibility while we are living to make decisions concerning our own passing. There are few greater gifts we can give to those around us than doing this hard work. The truth is, either we will make these arrangements before we die, or it will be done for us when we are gone, possibly along with the help of the government. (And we all know how great the government is at managing money.)

Many difficulties arise in families surrounding someone's death, but this almost always happens as a result of misunderstandings about the wishes and desires of the deceased. Sadly, these misunderstandings cannot be corrected in death, making it all the more difficult and thus illuminating the importance of clarity. The one who is going to a better place should take the lead in directing loved ones in what to do when he or she is not there. It would be selfish not to, actually. Knowing how difficult it will be for those around when you are gone (please don't question this), is it right that the hard decisions of how to handle the division of your property and/or possessions should accompany that already difficult grief?

Many of us have an unspoken fear that if we focus on

death, something might happen to us. We are afraid if we spend too much time talking about what happens when we are gone, then somehow that day might be a lot closer. But if my death goes anything like my life, then the fact that I'm prepared and ready means that nothing is going to happen to me for a long time.

I have found that to speak about our eventual deaths and to make plans accordingly actually helps banish fear, usher in courage, and bring comfort and security not only for us but most certainly for those we love as well. Even if they say something like, "Oh I don't want to talk about this," trust me, they will be so glad that you did. They don't know what they don't know yet.

Another reason we don't get our affairs in order is that it's overwhelming. We think, *I don't know yet where I want to be buried. How do I even know what things to decide right now? Who will be the one to take care of this? How would I place a value on all my stuff?* Well, let me say politely, if you can't make these decisions, think for a minute how hard it will be for someone else to.

There is no way to express how hard it is for a child (even if now an adult) to make decisions that he or she hopes the parents would have wanted to make, but the child just isn't sure. There is so much sadness already, and to question whether your parent wanted to be cremated or buried is an undue added burden that can be completely alleviated by one good discussion or document.

If we leave question marks where we could put periods in terms of our preferences, we have not given those who care about us the best chance to keep doing so in our death. Even if we don't know exactly what we want, it is better to fumble through making a decision than to leave things undecided. When you are free to get your affairs in order, you set those around you free to know they are caring for you in the best way they can.

Getting your affairs in order before your death is the only way you really have to communicate with and comfort people when you are gone. Have you ever been home when someone was away and found a little note or gift they tucked away for you to find when they were gone? Not only is it heartwarming, but it's a powerful experience—one I would want my loved ones to have when I am no longer here.

And because I am confident in my eternal home and released from the power of death, I am free to give this blessing to them.

Father, give us the freedom to get our affairs in order. Even grant us joy in the process, as we trust that we are caring for those we love by giving attention to these matters. And if our relationship with you doesn't bring us peace as we think of eternity, may that be our first order of business before moving on to disperse of the things we own.

Freedom to Fly

Patsy Clairmont

Oh, that I had the wings of a dove! I would
fly away and be at rest.

—Psalm 55:6 NIV

There they were—two huge orange butterflies outside my office window doing acrobatic feats in tandem. I decided to believe they had been sent to dance just for me. Although as I watched them weaving in and out of my flowering shrubs, I wasn't sure if they were flirting, fighting for territory, or just having a wing-ding of a good time—kind of a fluttery game of tag.

Whatever they were doing, it sure looked whimsical. I wished I could shed my work, don wings, and join them as they twirled about the neighborhood, alighting from time to time on daffodils and berry bushes. These majestic monarchs captured my desire to wing my way down the boulevards of life with beauty and grace.

Yesterday, my husband, Les, and I stopped for a red light and watched a small flock of blackbirds swoop across our vision and land in a nearby tree. Les asked, "Don't you wish sometimes that you could fly?"

Who hasn't wished it or dreamed of it? Just ask Wilbur, Orville, Amelia, or any of the astronauts.

There's just something about flight that translates to freedom, whether it's a butterfly, a bird, or a spaceship. Maybe it's the ease with which they move, the high places they can reach, and the joy they spread as they take flight, but they appear as creatures to be envied. What's not to want in, say, a butterfly's life—flight, nectar, allure, and freedom? Sounds pretty good to me.

Or not.

Did you know that the average life span for a butterfly is about seven days? Seven days! I've had colds last longer than that! The only butterfly with a longer life is a zebra butterfly, which can live up to ten months. But for other butterflies to attain the old-age status of the zebra butterfly, they would need to give up delectable nectar in order to imbibe sweat and chow down on dung. May I just say . . . ugh! With that kind of menu, maybe seven days is long enough to hang around.

Have you noticed that often what looks good from a distance when examined up close and personal is not the fragrant cup of azaleas it appears to be? The butterfly's brief stint and tissue-thin wings that leave it vulnerable to even a puff of wind give me pause. (I'm tipsy enough with my Reeboks cinched tight.)

Our neighborhood, besides being a haven for monarchs, has a large population and selection of birds, including Priscilla and Fritz. What? You say you've not heard of that breed? Well, actually Prissy and Fritz are ducks. Happily married mallards, I might add. I know this because they have been coming back to our little stream to have their family for several years. If they didn't like each other, wouldn't they just flap off in opposite directions? But instead, no matter how quackers they make each other, they hang in there together.

Every year, Prissy and Fritz choose a different site around our neighborhood to lay their ducklings. Last year it was in a neighbor's flowerbed. One day, a curious neighbor (no, it wasn't me this time) peeked into the nest while Prissy and Fritz were dipping their tails in the stream, and she counted twelve ducklings. Aw. No wonder the parents went for a dip; there had to be a lot of squawking going on in that nest!

I missed the family's first promenade because I went north for the spring. When I returned the following winter, though, I was told that only two of the babies survived and that the parents stayed with those two until they were grown. But between marauding hawks and ravenous turtles, the other ducklings were either gobbled up or drowned.

I hate that!

I know, I know, it's the balance of nature and all that

National Geographic jazz, but golly, who would want to hurt a little fuzzy quacker? Never mind, don't tell me, I know the answer, and yes, it's multiple choice.

Okay, now back to this flight thing. No wonder butterflies skitter fitfully; with only seven days to get all our travels in, we'd be erratic too. And ducks . . . well, they should learn to, uh, duck more often. Even with wings, they are vulnerable to hard-shelled enemies and harpooning hawks.

When I think about it, I guess we are all vulnerable like the monarch butterfly in that we don't know how long we've been given before our journey here is done. That makes me want to skitter about and do what's important . . . how about you?

And I do have from time to time a hard-shelled "enemy" enter my landscape. Not to mention the harpooning sarcastic remarks that can catch me off guard. We may have more in common with our feathered friends than we know.

A few days ago, I had a visit from a large flock of cedar waxwings. They converged on my red-berry-laden tree, where a frantic eating frenzy began. Within minutes the birds had stripped the tree bare, except for a few berries dangling from the lowest branches that weren't safe for them to get to. Then with a sudden flurry of wings, the bandit birds hightailed it to the safety of the big oaks before the hawks could get them.

It's not easy surviving in this world, is it? We have nature offering us a visual of both beauty and brutality. Not that we necessarily need a visual, since our lives often demonstrate both beauty and brutality in high definition.

My husband, Les, just came in from the grocery store. When he arrived at the front door, he found a group of women huddled around a baby dove that had fallen out of its nest. We could see the nest and mother above in the gutter, but we were helpless to change this sad tale. And the wings of the little one weren't strong enough to get him home to safety.

We gals can't help it; we just can't bear the injustice of that. We want to fix it. We want to liberate that baby bird from danger, to liberate the ducklings from their predators, and to liberate the sherbet-winged monarch wonders from their brevity, that they might pirouette across our landscapes eternally.

Girls, I checked my Bible concordance, and *fair* ain't there! But *liberty* and *freedom* are. Unfortunately, it's not up to us who goes free. We get to watch the stories unfold all around us, but we don't get to determine destinies.

Yet it really is a relief to not be in charge of this tilt-a-whirl planet full of people who often act as though they are off their axes. I mean what about Spiderman? No, not the comic-strip guy, but the fellow who regularly appears on newscasts illegally climbing the outside of skyscrapers. What's that about? Is that his attempt to take flight?

Or what about all the people who have barreled down the Niagara Falls? Ten people, including two women, have gone over the falls and lived. But why would anyone want to hurl down a 170-foot waterfall and then violently slam into the current below? Was that about sprouting imaginary wings and flying?

There must be an easier way.

Today, I watched a daddy help his little girl fly a kite. "Run, honey, run!" he urged, trying to help her gain momentum. "You can do it," he assured her. She giggled and ran harder out of a desire to please her daddy and to see the kite cartwheel across the sky . . . and I wonder if she didn't hope that, like the kite, she might fly too.

I don't know why we all seem to have tucked inside our hearts a desire to sprout wings and soar. But since it's inside us and we even dream about it, I wonder, I just wonder, if this longing isn't about that coming bright morning when we who love Christ will fly away?

Some glad mornin' when this life is o'er,
I'll fly away.
To a home on God's celestial shore,
I'll fly away.
I'll fly away, oh glory, I'll fly away.
When I die, hallelujah, by and by,
I'll fly away.
Just a few more weary days and then,
I'll fly away.
To a land where joy shall never end,

I'll fly away.
I'll fly away, oh glory, I'll fly away.
When I die, hallelujah, by and by,
I'll fly away.

Are you packed? You won't need much. There's no passport required for this flight because you won't ever have to prove your identity to anyone again. And feel free to leave your backpack of cares behind along with the pouch from your past, for this will be a whole new, monarch-winged beginning.

When we believe Jesus Christ died for us and we invite him to enter our lives, then our reservation for a flight that will be out of this world is a done deal.

Now tell me that doesn't set your heart aflutter!

Lord, you've tucked in my heart a longing for that
day when "hallelujah, by and by, I'll fly away." Help
me to be ready to soar!

Freedom For . . .

Freedom for Fulfillment

Barbara Johnson

> To everything there is a season, a time for every
> purpose under heaven: . . .
> A time to gain, and a time to lose; a time to keep,
> and a time to throw away.
> —Ecclesiastes 3:1, 6 NKJV

*O*ne thing about cancer: it frees you from all the unimportant stuff in your life. Suddenly, that two-page to-do list that's been burdening you all week is replaced by a couple of simple, overriding priorities: keep breathing and keep believing.

I've always been one who looks for the joy in whatever predicament I find myself in, so when I got the cancer diagnosis, I was determined to find something joyful in it. And sure enough, I discovered that I now have a great excuse for not doing all the things I didn't really want to do but for which I somehow ended up on the list of volunteers. Once you've been through a couple of rounds of chemo or a few doses of radiation, no one expects you to bring a casserole to the church's potluck or a plate of cookies to Bible study. You're completely excused from hostessing the garden club and can instead be a gracious guest and compassionately indulged moocher at just about any function you care to attend.

And then there's the freedom from fussing—with your hair, that is. You don't have to bother with cutting, coiffing, curling, or crimping your hair anymore because, if you're like most of us cancer survivors, you go through a stage where you don't *have* any hair. I opted for a wig I could send out to get cleaned and styled without ever having to drop my own head back into that uncomfortable beauty-shop shampoo sink. That was something to be joyful about, right there! I admire those spunky women who throw traditional style concerns to the wind and go topless (or maybe I should say wigless). Just think what fun these gals are to talk to; they show up everywhere with smiles on their faces, daring everyone to notice their shining heads, and immediately everyone in the room thinks, *That gal's gonna be the life of the party.*

And then there are those absent-minded types who appear without wigs unintentionally. One delightful speaker told a large women's gathering she hadn't really intended to give her presentation "in the bald," but it was winter, and she'd been wearing a ski cap around the house to protect her head from the cold. She'd gotten so used to the feel of the cap on her bald head that she was halfway to her destination when she realized, "I was in Memphis, and my hair was back in Little Rock."

Of course, at the same time it takes away the trivial stuff, cancer also steals some of the things that *are* important. Things like good health and happiness, for starters. And while I'm making light of it here, the truth is, I hate cancer. *Hate it.*

On the day cancer turned my life upside down and shook out all the clutter, I was stooped over in the laundry room, cleaning lint out of the clothes dryer. Talk about something trivial! Could *anything* be less important than dryer lint? Sometimes I think about how I spent the last "normal" morning of my life (or, at least, as normal as someone given my history of calamities could be), and I wish I'd been doing something a little more worthwhile—saving the world, perhaps, or spreading my joy somewhere. The story would so much more dramatic if I could say I was singing my heart out in the choir at a Billy Graham crusade or speaking to a love-filled Women of Faith audience when the tumor struck its first blow.

But no. I was eliminating lint.

Suddenly a strange feeling came over me, and I lost all the strength in my arms and legs. I oozed onto the laundry-room floor, and there I stayed for a couple of hours until my husband, Bill, came home from running errands. As I lay there—alert and pain free but with no more muscle tone than a wet noodle—it struck me as funny that I'd ended up on the *floor* after spending nearly thirty years operating Spatula ministry, an outreach that helped "scrape hurting parents off the *ceiling* with a spatula of love" when they landed there due to some heartache related to their adult children.

Hmm. Maybe I should start a new ministry and name it Dustpan for Despair or Ragmop the Ruins or Forklift of Faith, I thought to myself, wondering how many other moms found themselves sprawled on the laundry-room floor, emotionally or literally, without the means to get back on their feet again.

Eventually, Bill came home and helped me into a chair. I still had no pain or discomfort, only weakness, so it was awhile before family and friends convinced me I should go to the doctor. And the rest . . . well, the rest is often too hard to think about: surgery that revealed a malignant brain tumor, followed by a five-year stretch of tests, procedures, chemotherapy, bad diagnoses, and more pills than one person should ever have to pop.

Then, in the middle of my own cancer battle, the disease launched a totally unexpected sneak attack on Bill. Within six weeks of his diagnosis, he had moved on to heaven, and I felt like Wile E. Coyote in those silly Roadrunner cartoons when the coyote, outsmarted again, finds himself suspended in thin air after running off the edge of a cliff—right before he plummets to the bottom of the canyon and splats on the rocky ground.

Yes, cancer takes away the unimportant as well as the

important things—and people—in our lives. But in the process, it brings us freedom to focus entirely on what is *most* important.

When Martha complained to Jesus that her sister, Mary, was listening to Jesus rather than helping her prepare lunch, Jesus helped her get her priorities straight. He answered, "Martha, Martha, you are worried and upset about many things. Only one thing is important. Mary has chosen the better thing, and it will never be taken away from her" (Luke 10:41–42 NCV).

As this is written, I'm temporarily living in a convalescent center recovering from broken bones incurred in a fall. In my quiet room, it would be easy to succumb to self-pity and loneliness, concentrating on all that I've lost: my health, my husband, my mobility, my freedom to travel and share the message of love and hope that has been my life's work for thirty years. And to be honest, those dark moments do come. But recalling Jesus' words to Martha helps me end my pity party and remember that "only one thing is important."

Then it's just Jesus and me, and I know that my life has been emptied so he can fill it with his wondrous love and eternal promises.

Admittedly, I have to fight the impulse to complain, and I constantly wrestle to accept these circumstances I want to despise. But my goal is to recognize that my losses have given me a new freedom to fill my life with the one thing that is most important. Every day, I deliberately work toward filling my emptiness with the attitude of the apostle Paul, who wrote, "Since I know it is all for Christ's good, I am quite content with my weaknesses and with insults, hardships, persecutions, and calamities. For when I am weak, then I am strong" (2 Corinthians 12:10 NLT).

What comforting words those have been for me as I've recovered from this latest round of "weaknesses." There's nothing more encouraging, when you're bed-bound with broken bones, to realize that times of physical weakness free us to become stronger in our faith. It's taken awhile, but I've finally learned firsthand that when we're full of ourselves and our earthly priorities and schedules, there's no room for Jesus.

As hard as it's been for me to be emptied of my former life, I'm grateful for the gift I've been given in exchange: the freedom to be fulfilled by One who knows all about loss of liberty and leaving behind a pleasant lifestyle. If Jesus left paradise to suffer and die on earth for me, surely I have nothing to complain about when he frees me from life's clutter so I can focus on life's Creator.

Father, help me always to feel your strong, everlasting arms embracing me when life seems harsh and empty.

Freedom for Experiencing God's Love

Sheila Walsh

Now that you have made your souls pure by obeying the truth, you can have true love for your Christian brothers and sisters. So love each other deeply with all your heart. You have been born again, and this new life did not come from something that dies, but from something that cannot die. You were born again through God's living message that continues forever.

—1 Peter 1:22–23 NCV

Barry and I had been dating for over a year, and that night we were going to one of our favorite Laguna Beach restaurants. I love Italian food, and this restaurant had some of the best I have ever tasted. Deep inside me, there is a robust Italian woman longing to get out and share her pasta with the world.

I knew Barry would pick me up around seven o'clock, so I had just enough time to finish an essay for my C. S. Lewis class at seminary. I was in no great rush. We were far beyond the trying-to-look-perfect-on-every-date stage. (That lasted about four dates for me . . . too much work.)

Next time I looked at the clock, I saw it was almost seven. I changed out of my jeans and put on a dress. Now, I'm not much of a dress woman. My favorite uniform is blue jeans, a white shirt, and no shoes. However, if I do wear shoes, then they usually have four-inch heels. I believe it goes back to my primal fear of God calling me to be a missionary in lands with great hairy beasties. Subconsciously, I determined that if God was scanning the earth looking for good missionary stock, he would say, "Well, we can't send her. Look at her shoes!" So although dresses are not my thing, I made some concessions for Barry, who thinks that they look nice every now and then.

At seven on the dot, the doorbell rang. I opened the door, still struggling to get into shoe number two, and took a good look at him.

"You don't look well," I observed. "Are you feeling all right?"

"Yes! Sure! I'm fine," he replied, pacing the apartment like a woman with a wallet full of cash the day before Nordstrom's half-yearly sale.

"We don't have to go out," I offered. "I could cook something, and we could watch a movie."

"No! I mean . . . I'm fine. Really, I'm fine. Let's go."

It usually took fifteen minutes to drive from my apartment to downtown Laguna, but on a busy Friday night all bets were off. Barry seemed to be getting worse as we waited in traffic. I felt his forehead.

"You're hot," I said. "I think you might have the flu. It's going around, you know."

"Really, I promise I don't have the flu. I might throw up, but don't worry . . . I don't have the flu."

We finally found a parking spot and made our way into the bustling restaurant. Those novices without reservations had no hope, but Barry had planned ahead. We were shown to our table, and I remember thinking as I watched him sweat, *I wonder if he wants to break up with me? If he does, then I'm definitely having the tiramisu. Two of them!*

The waiter gave us our menus. I set mine down on the table for a moment, enjoying the boisterous Italian atmosphere.

"Aren't you going to order?" Barry barked.

"Man, you're cranky tonight," I said. "Here, have some bread. Your blood sugar must be low."

He glared at me. Finally, to avoid an international incident, I picked up my menu to look for the most fattening item. Cranky men do not deserve thin girlfriends. I couldn't understand the menu at first. There wasn't a cream sauce in sight. Then I realized that it wasn't a menu at all; it was a typed-out marriage proposal.

Sheila, will you marry me? I love you more than words can say.

I stared at the words for a moment. Then I looked up and found myself staring into a television camera.

"Am I on *Candid Camera*?" I asked.

"Well, answer him!"

The voice came from behind me. It was my best friend, Marlene. I suddenly realized that the restaurant was full of our friends, all waiting for my answer. I turned back to look at Barry, but he wasn't there. He was on his knees beside me holding out the most beautiful ring imaginable. There was a moment of silence. All eyes were on us.

"Yes!" I answered. "Of course I will marry you." Everyone cheered and clapped.

Later that evening, as Barry was dropping me off at my apartment, I asked him, "What would you have done if I'd said no? I mean, you had a camera crew, and all our friends were watching. It could have been mortifying!"

"You are worth the risk," he said simply as he kissed me good night.

Now we are twelve years into our marriage, and that restaurant-menu proposal is framed and hanging in our kitchen.

Today before I began writing, I read the passage in the apostle Peter's first letter to a church that was beginning to undergo suffering and persecution. I was particularly arrested by his command to "love each other deeply with all your heart" (1 Peter 1:22 NCV).

I often assume the commands in Scripture to love our brothers and sisters refer to those outside our own family circle. But Barry, as well as being my husband, is my brother in Christ. Every marriage goes through cycles. There are times when you feel very close and romantic and seasons where all that stops you from hitting each other over the head with a frying pan is the small child sitting at the supper table and smiling at you! Although romance in marriage ebbs and flows, the command to love each other deeply from the heart remains in place.

I spent some time with a woman recently at one of our conferences. She and her husband were struggling in their marriage. "I don't see why I should try to act in a loving way when he is so negative and unhelpful," she said. "He has put nothing in my heart for a long time, so if I'm running on empty, it's his fault."

I understood her position. When we feel that we are not valued or treasured, we tend to withdraw out of hurt. I shared with her that I believe we have been offered another way to live.

God's love is never conditional based on our behavior. He never looks at us and thinks that we need to lose ten pounds or would look better as a brunette. God sees each one of us as a priceless, beautiful treasure. He never runs out of love or withholds his love from us. I believe if we could hold this truth deep in our hearts, it would set us free to love.

I meet women all across the country every weekend. We are different ages and sizes, but one thing we all have in common is a deep desire for love that says, "You are worth-while. You are priceless. You are worth the risk." We have a deep well that we long to have filled with significance and a sense of belonging. We want to be cherished.

I don't know how romantic your life is or how many sweet moments and memories you have tucked into the satin pockets of your heart. But I know this: you are adored and cherished by God. Human romance is wonderful, but it comes and goes. God's passionate love for us never wanes. It's not affected by whether we are young or old, strong or weak. And the outlandish lengths to which God will go to prove his love are beyond any scheme a human being—even one as risky as my husband planned that night—could dream up.

It is my prayer for you this day that God, by his grace, will help you understand the depth, height, and measure of his love for you so that you will be free to love and to love deeply.

Father, help me truly believe today that you see me
as a beautiful, priceless treasure. Thank you for your
passionate, unconditional love for me.

Freedom for
Enjoying Life

Mary Graham

Command those who are rich in this present age not to
be haughty, nor to trust in uncertain riches but in the
living God, who gives us richly all things to enjoy.

—1 Timothy 6:17 NKJV

Luci Swindoll has been my teacher in many things,
but one thing I appreciate of all I've learned from
her is the study, history, and appreciation of art. I didn't grow
up in a place where art was taught in our local schools. In
college, I was required to take one course in art appreciation.
All I remember learning to appreciate is the end of the class.
I don't ever remember knowing anyone who knew very much
about art.

For one thing, I'm a very practical person. When I see a
need, I don't hesitate to dive in to see if I can help. That behavior is pretty predictable for me and has been since I was a
child. As a result, I've spent a good bit of my life . . . busy.
Even when there was no real reason to be busy at something

(anything!), I felt I should stay busy, if only in principle. So the thought of walking through a building for no other reason than to observe pictures hanging on a wall never crossed my mind. In fact, I considered some of those pictures absolute child's play and wondered what fool would paint such a scene—and, worse yet, who would buy it? To say I had no appreciation of art would be an absolute understatement. I was one of those people who, upon seeing a major piece of artwork by Picasso, for example, would think (or even say!), *A five-year-old could have done that.*

I had no knowledge of art and no interest in gaining understanding. I was content in my utter ignorance and had no desire to learn.

Then I met Natasha. Natasha was an English student at the University of Leningrad. I met her on her campus when I overheard her trying to pronounce the word *fireworks*. She and her friend were arguing over whether the emphasis should be on the first or second syllable. Being a practical person who busies herself about other people's business when perceiving an opportunity to help, I butted in to pronounce the word correctly. Both girls looked at me with utter shock. Their eyes were wide as they stared at me as if to say, "Who are you, what are you doing here, and why are you talking to us?"

Within a few minutes I discovered they were both English majors, and neither of them had ever spoken to anyone who spoke English as her first language. That made me about the coolest person on the planet at that moment. They immediately wanted to engage me in conversation—and, as it turned out, that English-language exchange continued over the next several years as I visited their campus time and again. In between those visits, we were constant correspondents.

At that time, Natasha and her friend lived in a country whose people enjoyed little or no freedom. I, on the other hand, was free to come and go anywhere I wanted and do whatever I pleased in my home country. We were each fascinated with the life and stories of the other. They would never ask me what they assumed were personal questions, such as what I did for a living and why, or where I was educated, or who my parents were. Those questions were considered rude. So they asked me things like, "How much did your purse cost?" "How often do you drink Vodka?" and (my favorite) "Do you have sex with your boyfriend?" These things were considered fair game in conversation and not at all inappropriate.

Starting with my first trip to their city, they took me to the Hermitage, one of the largest art museums in the world. As they gave me a tour through those halls, they explained every painting as if they were art teachers—and in many ways, they were. Only eighteen years old at the time, they'd grown up studying the great art of the world, much of which was owned by the Soviet Union.

Their knowledge of art astounded me; I could not keep up. I'd certainly never met teenagers who were such art connoisseurs and critics. What really caught my attention, however, was when we walked through room after room of paintings by Rembrandt, many of which had a biblical theme. These young girls knew nothing of the Bible or God. They'd never even seen a Bible and hadn't heard much about it except that its contents were worthless and trivial. Their interest in the Bible was nonexistent.

As they explained their perspective on various pieces of art dealing with stories I knew from the Bible, I found myself correcting them. "No, no. That is not about a painter whose son ran away. This painting depicts a story told by Jesus in the Bible. It's called the prodigal son." And I told them the story. And then the next painting, "No, no. That is not about a woman who seduced the gods. That is a painting of Mary Magdalene, whom Jesus forgave of her sins. The story is in the Bible." In time, these girls said that they would be very interested in reading the Bible since it was written about these paintings. "Can you give me a Bible?" Natasha whispered, knowing to have a copy of that book was forbidden in her country.

Those girls came to faith in Christ during our visit. When I returned home, my first call was to Luci. I begged her, "Will you please teach me everything there is to know about art?" She, of course, asked me for some sort of explanation for my sudden interest. I gave her the only one I had: I found a way to connect with students, and I wanted her to help me so I could help them.

That year, Luci and I made a trip from California to New York City. Every day we were there, we visited art museums. We had almost no money, but because I worked with a ministry, I was able to stay in a house owned by a mission agency for less than forty dollars a night. We flew to New York on our airline points, ate bagels and sandwiches on the street, and went to the museums at no charge. It's one of my favorite and most memorable vacations.

Since then, we've gone all over the world visiting art museums of every size and stature as Luci continues to teach me everything she knows about art. After only twenty-five years, we're certainly not there yet. In fact, we've not even scratched the surface.

Although my motive for becoming an art student was to reach out to somebody else, what has kept me in the study of art is something entirely different. What I have learned about people and life in general is amazing. What I've learned to enjoy is beyond explanation. What I've experienced in my relationship with Luci and many other friends now is extraordinary. What I thought I was doing for Natasha, God did for me.

I realize now that in my early years I permitted myself no freedom to really enjoy life. I learned to work, serve, help, and contribute. I focused on doing what I had to do. I was driven by obligation and accomplishment. I didn't really learn to live.

Now I know that God "gives us richly *all* things to enjoy" (1 Timothy 6:17 NKJV; emphasis added). As we enter into life and that richness, we grow even in our understanding of him. We limit ourselves, our relationships with others, and our relationship with God when we don't expand our hearts and minds. I'm reminded that Scripture even says, "And on the seventh day God ended His work which He had done, and He rested on the seventh day from all His work which He had done" (Genesis 2:2 NKJV). Even God had the freedom to stop working and do something restful.

But there's been a bigger purpose for me in resting from my work. It has to do with enrichment. As a result of knowing Luci and becoming a student of hers in my ongoing art education, a whole new world has been opened to me. That world has been enjoyable, but not just for my own sake. That world has broadened my perspective and made it possible for me to relate to people who care a lot about the things of this world and nothing about the God of this world. It's given me connectedness to a portion of the population that enables me to relate to them on a topic of interest to them. Once we find common ground, the conversation often leads to discussions of spiritual things.

Art is certainly not the only topic of interest to the general public. Some people love to talk about books, sports, fashion, music, garage sales, or eBay. People have a thousand points of connection. As believers, and ambassadors of Christ on earth, when we become conversational in something unrelated to spiritual things, that exchange can lead to deeper discussions, as my conversation with Natasha did.

Luci helped set me free to richly enjoy a great abundance of beauty that I never knew existed. And God gives me freedom for enjoying life and growing in those areas of beauty so that I might reach out to others, whether they speak my language or not.

God, thank you for giving us so many things in this world to enjoy. Help me use my hobbies and interests to connect with others in deeper discussions about you.

Freedom for God's Provision

Patsy Clairmont

Daniel was taken up out of the den, and no injury whatever
was found on him, because he believed in his God.

—Daniel 6:23b NKJV

When my friend Jan told me about a woman who was caring for a brain-damaged lion cub, I was curious to know how that had come about. I'm fascinated by what folks do with their energies and gifts. Later, Jan sent me the newspaper article about the story of Elizabeth and Daniel so I could read about it for myself.

Elizabeth, an artist who worked at a wildlife sanctuary, had been given the responsibility of caring for a lion cub named Daniel. Since he was brain damaged, Elizabeth had to teach him how to eat and how to make lion noises. Imagine. (I've been known to roar, but I'm not very lionlike. My kids might disagree, however, since I've almost eaten them for lunch a few times.)

Anyway, Elizabeth even helped Daniel learn to walk with support. But she said his favorite thing to do was to be rocked. Aw. Isn't that sweet? Unfortunately, when Daniel was thirteen months old, he died in Elizabeth's arms from a grand mal seizure.

I'm so glad Elizabeth was holding Daniel when he passed away. Even though he must have been an armful, I think that must have been comforting for him during his scary last moments.

Years later, Elizabeth painted a portrait of Daniel—and guess where she placed him? Up in a tree. Don't you love that? We all appreciate a much-needed boost when the limb is higher than we can reach. Since Daniel never could climb, it was Elizabeth's way to offer him a foot up.

Elizabeth's story reminds me of another Daniel who wasn't a lion, yet he sure got up close and personal with the big cats, and he was certainly given a foot up. He wasn't up a tree, but he was down in a pit. He was a beloved adviser to King Darius in the Old Testament, but when Daniel exercised his freedom to bend his knee to God in prayer each day, he was thrown into a den of hungry lions. What a jolt—from liberty to lions' lunch, all because you said your prayers. That would give one pause . . . or would it?

When they are behind bars, lions might look cute as cubs or like adorable, overgrown pussycats, but in reality those royal beasts can and will rip you apart in a heartbeat. Daniel,

I'm sure, looked like a filet mignon wrapped in a toga to that troupe of underfed, agitated, mistreated felines. But the next day, when the king approached the den and the stone was rolled away, you won't believe what happened. No, wait, instead of me telling you, why don't you go with the king and see for yourself?

> Then the king arose very early in the morning and went in haste to the den of lions. And when he came to the den, he cried out with a lamenting voice to Daniel. The king spoke, saying to Daniel, "Daniel, servant of the living God, has your God, whom you serve continually, been able to deliver you from the lions?"
>
> Then Daniel said to the king, "O king, live forever! My God sent His angel and shut the lions' mouths, so that they have not hurt me, because I was found innocent before Him; and also, O king, I have done no wrong before you."
>
> Now the king was exceedingly glad for him, and commanded that they should take Daniel up out of the den. So Daniel was taken up out of the den, and no injury whatever was found on him, because he believed in his God. (Daniel 6:19–23 NKJV)

Daniel walked out of the den the next day unscathed because God closed the mouths of the hungry, ferocious lions. That's amazing freedom. I'm sure Daniel's heart must have been ricocheting in his chest when he first stepped into the den, waiting to see what would happen, for even the most fearless of us can't predict God's plan. And even if Daniel was prepared to die, you have to admit being dismembered by wild animals would be a tad disconcerting.

After hours of safety, though, Daniel knew God was not only with him but had chosen to preserve him. How else could one explain what happened? No, there isn't any doubt who was holding Daniel in those scary hours.

If Daniel had painted a picture to commemorate his den experience, I wonder if it would have been one of bellowing ocher-colored lions held at bay by a holy hand; or maybe docile lions curled up at his dusty, sandal-clad feet contentedly purring as Daniel stroked their manes; or perhaps it would have been of the lions taking, what else, a catnap? The liberating truth is that God is not napping, and he is committed to our freedom.

Notice that God didn't prevent Daniel's struggle, but he was with Daniel in the midst of his struggle—just as surely as Elizabeth, the wildlife worker, was with her dear cub, overseeing his needs right up until his last breath.

Truth be told, as much as I appreciate knowing that God is with me during difficulties, what I really want him to do is rescue me before I have to face "the lions." "Don't make me go in the lions' den!" my heart cries. I'm not given to bravery. I want him to gather me into the safety of his arms and rock me into his security. Now, I know better than to believe that I can escape without persecution, injustice, and scary dens in my life, but it's still my leaning to avoid calamity whenever possible.

Yet hardship is often what it takes to cause my cub heart to become lioness strong. Difficulties are often what promote me to stay on the path so I don't wander into the weeds, looking for something that isn't there. It's through bouts of depression that I grasp the value of joy, it's in rejection that I learn compassion for others who hurt, and it's the jailor of judgment that teaches me about the invaluable key of liberty.

Speaking of keys, I wish I could have pitched one to Daniel's friends—Shadrach, Meshach, and Abed-Nego— when they were thrown into a furnace for refusing to worship an idol. Turns out they didn't need a key, because they had a Keeper. That day there were no lions after them; instead, the deafening roar came from a raging furnace fire.

It's inconceivable to me that people would throw other humans into a furnace, yet in the midst of the unimaginable God did the miraculous. The Lord literally walked in the fire with them and shielded the three faithful young men from harm.

Again, we see God did not spare his people from life-threatening circumstances but provided for them in the midst of their trials. It often takes hindsight to see God's hand of mercy when a tragedy strikes.

When my brother Don was killed in a car accident just

before his thirty-ninth birthday, we were stricken with the loss. In the days, weeks, and months that passed, as we were able to lift our heads above the tidewaters of our grief, we saw again and again God's benevolent hand of provision.

Sometimes when our ache is so great, it can temporarily blur our vision. Yet as the heavy fog lifts, we see that the Lord, by his very presence with us, opens up paths to freedom so we can bear up while we heal and so we don't have to live out our years under the dismal dictatorship of despair.

Remember the benevolent zoo worker Elizabeth? Well, she told of painting another lion that had lived his entire life caged. People, upon viewing the painting, felt she had made him look too fierce and scary, to which Elizabeth replied, "When I paint [captive] wild animals, I try to set them free."

Elizabeth was very Christlike in how she cared for the fragile cub Daniel—anticipating his needs, supporting his walk, teaching him lion noises, and offering him sanctuary in her loving arms. Her compassion is a broad-stroke painting of Christ's availability to us. Understanding God's provision for us in the midst of trials brings an inner freedom that will cause us to . . . yes, roar!

———

Lord, thank you for being with me in the midst of
my struggles. Reveal to me today your hand of mercy
and provision during my trials.

Freedom for
Believing God

Luci Swindoll

What good would it do to get everything you want
and lose you, the real you?
What could you ever trade your soul for?

—Mark 8:36–37 MSG

*I*t's amazing what we remember as we grow older. This morning I was looking at a small oil painting that hangs in my breakfast room and began to contemplate the friend who painted it—Anne Bradford. We were neighbors about forty years ago.

Anne was the spitting image of Diane Keaton. Same height, build, and demeanor. She dressed artistically; had a warm, winsome smile; and threw a witty mental curveball almost every time she opened her mouth. She was utterly delightful to be around! She made me laugh and think, always challenging me to explore new ideas. Anne was about ten years older than I, married to a man who designed systems for a large department store in Dallas, and they had one son, whom she called her "masterpiece."

Anne and I were reading *The Story of Civilization* about the same time and constantly compared notes about what we read. It's an eleven volume set by Will and Ariel Durant of unparalleled insight into the human condition . . . a very life-affirming revelation of history and human character.[5] We both loved these books. She was deep into volume eight while I was still on volume two. She told me she read each night and slid the book under the bed when she got sleepy, to take up the following night. "I don't ever want to be very far from those brilliant minds," she said. "They always bring me back to what's really important in life."

Anne loved opera, and during those days I was singing in the Dallas Opera Chorus. Occasionally, I invited her to a rehearsal or a performance. I always enjoyed her company. We talked about literature, art, music, travel, families, books, gardening . . . all the things that held a fascination for us both.

Perhaps the most noteworthy thing about Anne was that she had no interest at all in the things of God. I found this strange since she was so erudite, thoughtful, and rich in her spirit. She knew I was a believer in Jesus Christ, and while she never spurned the importance of him in my life, she had no place for him in hers. When I tried to talk to her about

Christ's redemptive plan of salvation, she responded with a very flat affect and a rather blank expression. I never pushed her to believe as I did or tried to coerce her into making a decision that wasn't truly genuine, from her own heart. I would simply share with her what the Bible taught and leave it at that. But we were worlds apart in the matter of our souls and remained that way for as long as I knew her.

Sadly, the most important thing in my life meant absolutely nothing to her.

One cold, winter night, Anne invited me and another friend to have dinner at her home. I was thrilled because I wanted to meet her family, see where she lived, and get a feel for her home life. When we arrived, Anne told us that her husband and son had left earlier to have a guys' night out while "the girls" had the run of the house. Her home was small, very tidy and artistic, immaculately furnished, and extremely inviting. There was a roaring fire in the fireplace, and she had moved a small dining table in front of a window and had carefully set it with her finest china, a bottle of French red wine, and a candle, the glow of which I could see as we pulled up out front.

There was a fierce wind blowing outside, and because the limbs of the trees were bare, I remember hearing them scratch the windowpanes over and over. Ice was forming, and the twigs of the limbs etched their marks onto the glass. It was a setting I've never forgotten.

When we were all seated at the table, our conversation turned to the subject of art, which it often did. Each of us was buying various small pieces of original art at the time. We all watched for sales and called one another when something interesting appeared on the horizon of our lives.

That particular evening our conversation turned to Kathe Kollwitz, the German expressionist printmaker. Some of her etchings had turned up for sale a few weeks before, and I had bought a self-portrait (which still hangs on my wall today). We were especially interested in Kollwitz because of all she had endured during the Second World War at the hands of the Third Reich. Kollwitz was a simple woman, a wife and mother who was highly gifted as an artist. She was a respected, well-loved craftsman and teacher who survived the domination of the Gestapo; the loss of her job at the Academy in Berlin; the deaths of her husband, son, and grandson; the interrogation of the Nazis; and the ultimate rejection of her art. Her block prints and etchings revealed sympathy for the common person and the remarkable strength of the human spirit under pressure.

Kollwitz was a testimony to the three of us women as we sat around the table that night. Her life spoke of the importance of character. We discussed her ability to withstand suffering and loss. We talked about how life is full of sorrows and heartache and queried how any of us can go through that much loss without totally giving up. I mentioned there was no way to explain it except that God made it possible. I said something like, "Kollwitz had to find the freedom in her spirit to let go of all those losses or she couldn't have endured such agonies. I don't think it would have been possible."

Anne looked at me and made the most interesting comment: "You know, Luci, one day down the road . . . let's say ten years . . . you won't believe in God either. When you're older and wiser in the ways of the world, God will mean nothing more to you than a figment of your imagination. If you want to be free of anything, you have to set yourself free. He doesn't exist, and the sooner you realize that, the stronger you'll be inside. That's the way it works."

Even though that was forty years ago (at least), I have thought of that statement numerous times. And that night. I've heard in my head over and over the branches etching their marks into the icy windowpane and remembered Anne's words: *One day down the road . . . let's say ten years . . . you won't believe in God either.*

I have no idea where Anne is or if she's still serving dinner guests off that little table in her cozy, inviting living room. I don't know who her friends are or who she's discussing art or music or travel or books with these days. Or even if she's still living. I can't speak for her except to ask what Jesus asked in Mark 8:36–37: "What good would it do to get everything you want and lose you, the real you? What could you ever trade your soul for?" (MSG).

The truth is, as much as I loved Anne, respected her as a person, and admired how she reflected upon and processed life, the statement she made to me that night could not have been further from the truth. I've often wondered why she said it. Where did it come from inside her? Was it for me to hear or for her own heart?

A lot about me has changed since the mid-1960s. My views have altered on issues about life. I've learned more about the world. I've grown more tolerant of people and their circumstances. I've realized I don't have to prove everything I believe. But other things are just like they were back then. I'm still collecting art, still plowing my way through the Durants' *Story of Civilization*, still enjoying a winter's evening with friends . . . but most of all, I still believe in God. More than ever.

You know how I know that? Because I have peace about God in my heart. His Spirit rings true with my spirit, and he has kept his word over and over. There is a validation inside that can't be had if belief is not present. I've learned the truth about God, and that truth has set me free—free to be me, free to love him, free to live fully by his grace.

I can't really explain this freedom he's provided . . . not to me and certainly not to Anne. I just know I feel it deeply and love the fact of that feeling. My relationship with God has been tested and deepened and lengthened and enhanced through living, suffering, aging, losing, and loving . . . all that and more. He's very much there, strong in my heart, mind, and spirit. We're hanging out together all the time, he and I.

I know all that about me for sure. And I trust it's now true about my friend Anne.

———

Father, I choose to believe the truth about you and to
experience the freedom you provide as I live fully by
your grace for the rest of my life.

Freedom for Grace

Marilyn Meberg

Since we have been made right in God's sight by faith,
we have peace with God because of what Jesus Christ
our Lord has done for us.

—Romans 5:1 NLT

wo months ago, I was stopped in Plano, Texas, for
speeding. The policeman said he clocked me going
thirty-eight miles per hour in a restricted zone where the
speed limit is twenty-five. When he first asked me if I knew
I was going thirty-eight miles per hour, I thought maybe he
was going to congratulate me; I can't remember the last time
I was only going thirty-eight miles an hour.

The policeman made my breaking of the law abundantly
clear to me. I was then put on restriction for three months.
That meant should I get another speeding ticket during my
time of restriction, it will appear on my record and be sent to
my insurance company. If I don't break the law again during
restriction, my insurance company will not be notified. I

have been serving out my time very conscientiously. It helps, of course, that since my back surgery I am not allowed to drive for a month. There is no doubt that keeping me off the streets is good for my driving record.

But what if the policeman who stopped me approached my car smiling warmly, extended his hand, and said, "Hello, Marilyn Meberg. How nice to see you"? I would have been thrown off balance by his manner. And what if, as I handed him my driver's license and proof of insurance, he said, "Oh I know you, Marilyn . . . I don't need to see your license. In fact, I know you so well that I even know the numbers of hairs on your head. You, Marilyn, are a treasure and you always will be."

I would instantly assume there was something deviant about this policeman and yet again regret that I continue to bear the burden of being a sixty-six-year-old sex symbol. If then he said that with the speeding ticket came a substantial fine but that he would take care of it at no cost to me, I might dial 9-1-1 for protection.

What would be strange to me about this policeman's behavior is that it is not how the system works. I broke the law. I was guilty. I needed to face the consequences and not make the excuse that I was listening to Dr. Laura on the radio and her often-brutal answers to people make me so mad that I press on the gas pedal. Instead, I would need to meekly take my ticket, pay it, and go on restriction for three months.

There is something comforting to our inner sense of justice

when we pay the consequences for our misdeeds. It is not that we love consequences. Many of us even go out of our way to avoid them. Nevertheless, the internal judge and jury system that are sequestered in the chambers of our soul must be satisfied; justice must be served. When justice is served and punishment received, our relief becomes our reward. That explains why it is so difficult for us to understand and accept the doctrine of grace. Grace means I don't pay for my wrong deeds. Jesus did that instead.

In addition to our need to pay the consequences of our sin and our baffled response to the message that Jesus already did it, there is another human quandary thrown into the mix. We assume that when we sin, God becomes angry with us. *Why wouldn't he?* we think. Here's another mind-boggling truth: God does not get mad at us when we sin. Now, I have to admit that fact really throws me off balance.

Thirty years ago, little Beth Meberg came trudging in the house one afternoon, thus concluding another harrowing day in the second grade. She threw her stuff down in the "stuff corner" and wordlessly walked down the hall, went into her room, and closed the door. Of course I was curious. I waited a couple of minutes and then knocked on her door.

"Baby, what are you doing in there? You didn't even say hi to me when you came home."

"I know, Mama. I didn't say hi 'cause you're mad at me."

"Why am I mad at you?"

"'Cause I hit Bobby Ditmore at recess and had to go to the principal's office 'cause of fighting on the playground."

"Why did you hit him?"

"'Cause I don't like him and never have."

As I took a second to process this behind-the-door conversation, Beth said, "See? I told you you were mad at me!"

When I gained access into Beth's room, she confessed it was not the first time she had hit Bobby, but it was the first time she had to go to the principal's office because of it. I tried to get to the bottom of why this freckle-faced child of ours had become such a pugilist. Why would she knock Bobby Ditmore down just because he got on her nerves? She had no good reason except to say some people need to get knocked down sometimes. I couldn't stifle a giggle on that one, which Beth interpreted as evidence I was not mad and could then be released from her self-imposed restriction.

I assured Beth that I was not mad at her but that I was disappointed. We had a chat about kindness and behavior that we do because it's the right thing to do and not the thing we necessarily want to do. I couldn't tell if the ethics of the whole conversation penetrated her consciousness or not. She was just relieved to know that Mama was not mad.

Generally, no one wants to make Mama mad. By the same token, no one wants to make Daddy mad either. In fact, we rarely want anyone to be mad at us. It threatens our security and sense of safety if someone is mad. There are many of us who live by the philosophy of "peace at any price." Why? It makes our environment less threatening.

The same reasoning applies to our emotions about God. If our mama's anger threatens us, imagine what God's anger makes us feel. He could wipe all persons off the face of the earth. That thought alone raises huge security issues. There is no doubt he has the power to do whatsoever he chooses. For example, read this powerhouse verse:

> But God made the earth by his power,
>   and he preserves it by his wisdom.
> He has stretched out the heavens by his understanding.
> When he speaks, there is thunder in the heavens.
> He causes the clouds to rise over the earth.
> He sends the lightning with the rain
>   and releases the wind from his storehouses.
> Compared to him, all people are foolish
>   and have no knowledge at all! (Jeremiah 10:12–14 NLT)

But the question here for us is not, "Is God powerful?" The question is, "Does God get mad at us when we sin?" We know God hates sin; Scripture makes that abundantly clear. For example, Psalm 90:8–9 says, "You spread out our sins before you—our secret sins—and you see them all. We live our lives beneath your wrath. Ending our years with a groan" (NLT).

How then can we possibly say that God does not get mad

at us when we sin? Here's the reason: Jesus took upon himself all sin; every single sin that sets off the wrath of God, Jesus took on himself and carried it to the cross. When Jesus hung on the cross, slathered with our sin, God turned away from him. Jesus experienced the judgment of God, which was total rejection and abandonment. All the wrath of God for sin was poured out on Jesus. And when the death price for sin was paid, God reclaimed his Son.

God has no more anger for us and our sin. Well, that's a leap, isn't it? Romans 5:1 states, "Since we have been made right in God's sight by faith, we have peace with God because of what Jesus Christ our Lord has done for us" (NLT). Being made right with God is being made perfect because of Jesus. God now sees us as perfect—not because we never sin but because Jesus died for that sin, and God sees us through the perfect person of Christ.

So what about all those verses that describe how God will judge us and punish us for sin? What about Psalm 90:9, which says we live beneath the wrath of God and our lives end with a groan?

When Jesus made us perfect, God's wrath was extinguished. When Jesus made us perfect, our lives changed from groan to grace.

Hear it again:

He doesn't treat us as our sins deserve,
nor pay us back in full for our wrongs!

As high as heaven is over the earth,
    so strong is his love to those who fear him.
And as far as sunrise is from sunset,
    he has separated us from our sins. (Psalm 103:10–12 MSG)

Does God still hate sin? Of course. But because of Jesus, he does not hate us or react toward us in anger.

Because the anger of God was put on Jesus and now is no longer on us, do we just kick up our heels with no responsibility for our sinful choices? Galatians 5 gives us this warning: "It is absolutely clear that God has called you to a free life. Just make sure that you don't use this freedom as an excuse to do whatever you want to do and destroy your freedom" (v. 13 MSG).

Our freedom is lost through poor choices. Grace keeps it from being lost forever, but our choices determine the richness of our walk with God.

Let's wrap up our discussion with this great advice from Ephesians 3: "God can do anything, you know—far more than you could ever imagine or guess or request in your wildest dreams! He does it not by pushing us around but by working within us, his Spirit deeply and gently within us" (v. 20 MSG).

—

God, thank you so much that you are not angry with me because of my sin. Help me make wise choices as I walk each day in the freedom you have given me through Jesus Christ.

Freedom for God's Kingdom Work

Thelma Wells

> I delivered to you first of all that which I also received:
> that Christ died for our sins according to the Scriptures,
> that He was buried, and that He rose again the
> third day according to the Scriptures.
>
> —1 Corinthians 15:3–4 NKJV

For more than forty years, my family has made a big deal out of Easter. Well, it *is* a big deal. Easter is the most important holiday of the year—the day that signifies the resurrection of our Lord and Savior, Jesus Christ. It lives out the familiar Scripture John 3:16: "For God so loved the world that He gave His only begotten Son, that whoever believes in Him should not perish but have everlasting life" (NKJV).

Love is the optimum word for my family. For us, Easter is an entire weekend of friends, family, and fun wrapped up in love. It goes like this. We plan what we're going to eat. (Food is very important at holidays, you know.) Usually we plan the meat first, like ham, chicken, ribs, or roast. Then we build the vegetables around the meat inspiration. Cabbage, black-eyed peas, okra gumbo, greens or green beans, and macaroni and cheese usually make the menu. If I don't have parker house rolls and butter, something is missing. Okay, I make cornbread too.

But nothing is better than my secret iced tea drink. No, I won't tell you how I make it. It's a secret.

The most important plans, according to the thirty-plus children who land in my front yard after Sunday morning service, include the coloring, stuffing, hiding, and hunting of the Easter eggs. The child with the most eggs wins the hunt and gets a gift.

If you think we believe Easter is just about family, friends and fun, let me assure you, we don't. Amid all the chaos of the Easter festivities, I teach the truth about Easter and the symbols of Easter, such as:

- The egg represents the tomb from which Jesus rose.
- The lily represents the resurrection of hope.
- The bunny represents new life during springtime.
- The lamb represents the Lamb of God, who takes away the sin of the world.
- The angel represents the power of God to roll away the stone.
- The cross represents the crucifixion of Christ.
- The heart represents where Jesus lives today, within the heart of man. He is risen indeed!

The most powerful part of the Easter story is that Jesus loves us so much he gave his life in order to save us from eternal death. "Therefore the Father loves me, because I lay down My life that I may take it again. No one takes it from Me, but I lay it down of Myself. I have power to lay it down, and I have power to take it again. This command I have received from my Father" (John 10:17–18 NKJV).

What did Jesus accomplish by dying on that cross? He demonstrated his love for us and freed us from the penalty of our sins. Because we experience freedom through Jesus' death, we are free to fulfill our purpose in life without guilt and shame. In other words, Jesus' death freed us so we could live without unnecessary constraints.

Many people are looking for absolute freedom. Freedom from fear, anxiety, sickness, hopelessness, poverty, ignorance, negative emotions, insecurity, disharmony, joblessness—you name it, we want freedom from it. But we cannot experience complete and total freedom without some constraints. To be free to do whatever we want is to become a slave to laziness and sin.

Our purpose in life is not to shun our responsibilities as model citizens or to become lazy about any other obligations, but to be free to live out our God-given assignments. Jesus knew his purpose well: he came to set the prisoners free.

Hundreds of years before Christ walked this earth, Isaiah prophesied clearly what the Messiah's purpose would be:

The Spirit of the Lord God is upon Me, because the Lord has anointed Me to preach good tidings to the poor; He has sent Me to heal the brokenhearted, to proclaim liberty to the captives, and the opening of the prison to those who are bound; to proclaim the acceptable year of the Lord, and the day of vengeance of our God; to comfort all who mourn, to console those who mourn in Zion, to give them beauty for ashes, the oil of joy for mourning, the garment of praise for the spirit of heaviness; that they may be called trees of righteousness, the planting of the Lord, that He may be glorified. (Isaiah 61:1–3 NKJV)

Christ's purpose was the kingdom's work—that is, the work of helping people on this earth. Since we are supposed to emulate Christ, we can join him in the same purpose: to encourage the poor, to speak healing to the brokenhearted, to show the freedom of Jesus to those who do not believe, to enlighten those who are in darkness, to let them know that Jesus lives in our hearts, to be a comfort to those who are hurting and grieving, to spread joy wherever we go, and to praise God in all situations so that people will see the Savior living in us. Christ sent us to be ambassadors for him on earth to help bring others into his kingdom.

God wants us to serve his purpose on the earth and to live with him forever when we die. That's the freedom he gave us on the morning he arose from the grave. That's the reason Easter is so extra special.

Jesus lives today within the hearts of those who love him. Yes, he is risen indeed! And because he lives in our hearts, we can freely do the work of his kingdom, knowing that we "can do all things through Christ who strengthens [us]" (Philippians 4:13 NKJV).

My wish for you is that God's love renews your spirit and fills your heart with hope and happiness as you celebrate the amazing freedom to carry out God's kingdom work.

Jesus, you are risen indeed! Thank you for the freedom you provided through your death and resurrection. Help me today to fulfill my purpose by doing the work of your kingdom!

Freedom for Following New Trails

Barbara Johnson

I will walk about in freedom, for I have
sought out your precepts.

—Psalm 119:45 NIV

*W*alking by faith, not by sight, is something Kim Taylor has done for years. Twenty-six years, as a matter of fact. Kim has been blind all her life—since she was born two months prematurely, weighing only two pounds. Given that rough start, she's done remarkably well, and today she lives a rewarding, active life in Florida.

One of my friends met Kim; her guide dog, Rufus; and her friend Sheila Jones at a Women of Faith conference. I love the story Kim shared about the freedom Rufus has given her.

Rufus spent the first year of his life with a puppy raiser, then he went to guide-dog school for six months, where he learned forty commands. Now that he and Kim are a team, she has taught him several more essential skills, including finding the Slurpee machine at 7-Eleven stores!

What a wonderful story Kim tells about the expanded freedom she's enjoying now that she has the devoted Rufus by her side. It began with what Kim calls "the first walk." Here's how she described it:

One of the first things you do as you go through training with your guide dog is to walk a trail you've never been on before. If you've been accustomed to using a white cane, you generally walk pretty slowly, tapping the ground in front of you to make sure there's a place to step. But that morning during our training, the trainer took us to this new trail, and I put my hand on Rufus's harness—and it felt like I was flying down that path. I was going faster than I'd ever gone before. It was amazing, this totally new experience, and I wasn't a bit scared. I'd learned that I could trust Rufus, and I flew down that path laughing and gasping and just about overwhelmed with all the feelings that were bubbling up in me.

At the end of the trail, there was a bench, where we stopped to rest. I sat down beside the trainer who'd been waiting for me there. I praised Rufus—and then I burst into tears. I cried and cried and cried. The trainer said, "Are you okay?" But I couldn't talk. It was all just too . . . I don't know, it was just too wonderful.

Later another trainer said to me, "I heard you cried when you finished the new trail. Is anything wrong? Do you want a different dog?"

I laughed and said there was no way anyone was taking Rufus away from me. I had cried out of the sheer joy and happiness over the freedom Rufus had given me. It was a wonderful illustration of how, when we walk by faith and not by sight, God gives us a wonderful new freedom to do things we could never have done before. We don't have to be afraid, knowing he's there. We can venture out; we're freed to try new things for his glory.

Hearing Kim's story, I remembered how faith had freed me to launch the outreach ministry Bill and I operated for thirty years. Unofficially, it began when our son Steven was killed in Vietnam. Seeking to share God's comfort with other hurting families who had lost someone in that war, we contacted those whose names appeared in the casualty lists published in local newspapers. Our work continued when another son, Tim, was killed by a drunk driver. Then, when we discovered that another son, David, was a homosexual, we expanded our outreach to families who were struggling to cope with their own children's homosexuality as well.

When we first learned that David was gay, I looked for help and couldn't find any. In my distress, I prayed urgently to God, begging him to help me survive the ordeal I was facing and promising that if he would get me through it, I would start a ministry to help other hurting parents. (As I've said many times, I really didn't think I *would* survive it, and, you know, most of us will promise God anything when we think we're teetering on the edge, peering into that chasm called death.)

As the days passed and I realized I wasn't going to succumb to despair, it occurred to me that maybe God was keeping his end of our "deal" and that he expected me to keep my part of the bargain too. I had no idea how to start a "real" ministry, but just as Kim did, I gave God my hand—and hung on for all I was worth. And that's how Spatula Ministries has survived all these years as he has led me down one new trail after another.

It's interesting how God puts those new trails in front of us. It took Ann Fisk, another Women of Faith friend, nearly five years to recognize where God seemed to be leading her. For a long time, Ann, who lives in Houston, suffered a variety of health problems, including asthma, severe allergies, and sleep apnea. She was treated by all sorts of doctors and underwent fourteen surgeries, including two major operations. "And both of those times, I quit breathing while I was on the operating table," she said.

Despite all the different treatments, her problems continued. She was able to keep her job, but throughout the long ordeal, she felt completely exhausted. Whenever she wasn't at work, she was sleeping. "I never had enough energy for anything else. For five years, I really couldn't go anywhere but work and home. I just wasn't able," she said.

Ann's daughter, Kari, was praying constantly for her mom. "I prayed so hard that God would guide her in knowing what to do," Kari said.

Every day, on her way to work, Ann drove by the same doctor's office. It turns out God had been guiding her by that doctor's office for several years, but Ann never "got it" until one day, out of the blue, she found herself copying down the doctor's phone number.

The doctor ran several tests and then referred her to a cancer doctor, who sent her to a sleep clinic where she was diagnosed with chronic obstructive pulmonary disease. Her next appointment was with a lung specialist.

"He walked into the exam room and introduced himself," Ann said. "And then, without examining me or doing any tests, he said, 'You have to go on oxygen—today.'"

Ann was about to experience the same amazing freedom Kim had felt when she put her hand on Rufus's harness and trotted down that unfamiliar trail for the first time. Once Ann's body started getting the oxygen she needed, a whole new life opened before her.

"It's hard to believe I went through all that I did, and no one thought simply to put me on oxygen," she said. "Now my oxygen tank is my baby. I take it everywhere (I have a small, portable unit that I can carry in a bag)—and I really do go *everywhere*."

Less than four months after she went on oxygen, Ann flew to California to celebrate Thanksgiving with her family. And as she gained strength and stamina, Kari noted, her mother's faith "was growing along with her energy."

Ann shared her story with my friend during a Women of Faith conference in Houston, where she and Kari—and the bag containing Ann's small oxygen bottle—joined the other thousands of women singing and praising God with love, laughter, and *energy*.

There was a time when Ann refused to park in handicapped spots—"until the day came when I *had* to park there," she said. She now recognizes that she does have a disability, but she has continued working at her job throughout her medical problems and now sings in the church choir, enjoys a variety of other rewarding activities, and happily states that "thanks to good medical treatment and my portable oxygen supply, I'm constantly on the go."

Kari has been amazed by the transformation she's seen in her mother: "Her energy for life and in her faith in the Lord has been amazing to watch."

"I wouldn't wish this problem on anybody," Ann noted, "but what I've learned from it is that God has seen me through it—and I know he'll help me get through anything else that comes my way."

Ann hopes others will be inspired by her story, especially one acquaintance who has watched her go from being housebound to enjoying her newfound freedom. "She has a similar problem, but she told me she's too embarrassed to wear the oxygen line and take the tank around with her. It just floors me that she's lost six years of her life because she doesn't want to be seen as someone who needs a little help to live a full life," she said.

What's holding you back from enjoying the full and free life God intends for you? Are you ignoring what you need to overcome emotional or physical barriers? Remember that joke about the man who stood on the roof of his flooded home and refused offers of help from several would-be rescuers, insisting, "God will save me"? The man eventually drowned. When he got to heaven, he said, "Lord, I trusted you. Why didn't you save me?"

God looked at him in exasperation and answered, "What are you talking about? I sent a rescue swimmer, a boat, and a helicopter, and you wouldn't go!"

God's gifts make us "free indeed," as Jesus said in John 8:36 (NIV). But sometimes we have to put forth a little effort to find and feel those gifts at work in us, understanding that they may lead us down new trails we've never traveled before.

Jesus, I want to follow where your love desires
to take me. Lead on, Lord!

Freedom for a Childlike Faith

Luci Swindoll

Unless you accept God's kingdom in the
simplicity of a child, you'll never get in.

—Mark 10:15 MSG

ecently in church, the children's choir sang "My God Is Mighty" and "This Is My Father's World." There must have been eighty adorable children on risers singing their little hearts out. Hand motions and all, they were wonderful. Several waved to their parents, scratched their noses, stood on one foot and then the other . . . but all were very dressed up and looking their best. Little boys wore ties, and many of the girls had on sparkly dresses. (My great niece, Jessica, sang in that choir and happened to be the slowest-moving child on the planet as the choir exited. She waved and waved as if she were the Rose Bowl queen!)

One little girl in particular held my attention. She sang heartily and didn't hold anything back when it came to putting into motion the might of our God or the fact that the w-h-o-l-e world belongs to Him. Her broad gestures told all of us that she truly believed what she was singing. Dressed in a long, frilly pink dress with a matching bow in her hair, she looked adorable. Each time the music stopped after a song, she *curtsied*! It wasn't just a bow; it was a full-fledged curtsy. She was the only child to do it, as though she'd been assigned the task and wanted to perform it well. My friends all commented on how sweet that was. Each of us was smiling as we enjoyed the moment.

Nobody ever curtsies anymore. The last time I saw it was at the opera when the prima donna took a deep bow onstage just before the curtain dropped, to acknowledge respect for the audience and appreciation for our thundering applause.

But one child in church in a group of eighty? Never.

What impressed me most was that this little girl felt free to be herself, no matter what. No matter who was looking. None of the others followed suit, but that didn't bother her. She felt like curtseying, so she did. Maybe her parents taught her to do that after a performance, or maybe she saw a movie in which someone curtseyed to royalty; but whatever the source, she wasn't embarrassed, reluctant, or afraid to stand alone. Like our little Rose Queen Jessica, she was free and every one of us in the audience was moved by her freedom of expression. There were smiles on every face.

Wouldn't it be wonderful if we were all that comfortable

in our own skin? If we were free to express things our way without fear of reprisal or correction? I don't mean lawless or rude behavior—stepping over the boundaries of a normal life—but living out a genuine vitality that enables us to experience spontaneous freedom at our core. I'm talking about enjoying the life God designs for each of us individually. We wouldn't be copies; we'd be originals . . . sharing childlike expressions of life and love, uninhibited and free, without wondering what others might think.

The great German educator and founder of the kindergarten system, Friedrich Froebel, once said, "The child-soul is an ever-bubbling fountain in the world of humanity." It's a constant source of refreshment to everybody.

During the years my father lived in an assisted-care facility, I went to see him every day. On Sunday afternoons, young parents would come to visit their aging loved ones. When their children arrived, "an ever-bubbling fountain" began to overflow. Joy was everywhere. People laughed, talked, asked the kids questions, listened to their answers, and were visibly cheered up by their presence. Nobody changed the mood of that place like little children freely being themselves. The children could talk about anything that came to mind, and we all listened with interest.

I have a friend in Florida who works with the children of her Christian friends, teaching them to write and give their own testimonies about how they came to know Christ personally.

She does a remarkable job with these youngsters, all under the age of eleven. I asked her once what procedure she goes through to get them to talk about their faith.

"Well," she said, "I take them out to eat first, then we just visit. I try to make them feel comfortable and free. I ask questions and write down what they say."

"What are some of your questions?"

"Simple things. How would you introduce yourself to someone? What kinds of things do you like to do? How does it feel to live in your family? What do you like most about being the oldest (or youngest) . . . and what do you like the least?"

After establishing a rapport with the child, she probes deeper into the part about faith: "How did you first hear about God and his love for you? How would you say you became a Christian?"

All the while the child is talking, my friend continues to write down everything. From that, she chooses the words that go into what she calls the "nugget" . . . the child's testimony. "I end the conversation by asking what they pray for and what they need God to help them with. If they have a favorite Bible verse, we close with that and it becomes part of the nugget."

There may be a need for clarification on some things, but for the most part, everything is in the words of the child. My friend reads back to the children what they've said just to be sure it's exactly what they meant. She asks them to copy it in their own handwriting, takes their picture, and puts the two together for the finished piece. In the end, they wind up with a sheet of paper with their picture and their story . . . ready to share with somebody else. The whole testimony is between three to five minutes long. (Generally speaking, the most powerful stories are short anyway, so what better time to learn that than when we're children?)

I had never heard of anyone teaching this to children before. It's brilliant. It guides children into personal thoughts that matter most and helps them see who gave them real freedom. When they stand in front of their Sunday school class or even their families, they have confidence in telling their story because they know exactly what to say. More than that, for the rest of their lives, it secures in their minds the reality of their relationship with Christ and how it began.

Let me share one of those sweet testimonies with you, in the child's own words:

My name is Karin Sastre. I am eight years old and I am in second grade. The thing I like best about my family is when we do things together. We love on each other a lot, and we go on family vacations.

I do lots of activities, and I am a Brownie. I also sing and take lessons. A while ago, my family went to Beach Fest. That day I heard a guy speak about not knowing who God is. It made me sad because if we don't know

God we will not go to heaven. In heaven, there is no sadness and the streets are made of gold. Jesus wants all of us to be in heaven one day with him.

That day, I asked Jesus to come into my heart and forgive my sin. Sin is when I hit my brother or get in trouble. Jesus forgives me—and died on the cross for me. I wanted to get baptized because I am a Christian. I studied many verses about God, and he is helping me learn self-control.

My favorite verse that I have memorized is John 3:16: "For God so loved the world that he gave his one and only Son that whoever believes in him shall not perish but have eternal life."

We read in Mark 10:13–16 about children coming to Jesus; but when they arrived, the disciples rebuked the people who brought them. "Jesus was irate and let them know it: 'Don't push these children away. Don't ever get between them and me. These children are at the very center of life in the kingdom. Mark this: Unless you accept God's kingdom in the simplicity of a child, you'll never get in.' Then, gathering the children up in his arms, he laid hands of blessing on them" (vv. 14–16 MSG).

That's a very clear mandate. In order to get into the kingdom of God, we must have a simple, straightforward, childlike trust in Christ Jesus and what he did for us on the cross.

We can learn a lot from children. In their unpretentious way, they have an amazing impact on us. When freedom of expression is not allowed, the gift of transparency is denied. That's also true in adults. When the spirit of self-expression is squelched, it's easy to get locked into a way of life that holds us captive to fear.

Be comfortable in your own skin and see what happens. And don't forget to curtsy. Remember, when you're free in Christ, you're free indeed.

———

God, help me to have a childlike faith and love for you that is uninhibited and free, without wondering what others might think.

Freedom for a Full Life

Patsy Clairmont

The righteous will flourish like a palm tree. . . .
They will still bear fruit in old age,
they will stay fresh and green.

—Psalm 92:12, 14 NIV

I think a strong wind must have caught the pages of my calendar, causing years to haphazardly stockpile. Am I really that, ahem, well-seasoned? Last year that accumulation resulted in a swarm of candles, similar to a raging brush fire, storming across my birthday cake and singing my pride. Why, the three-layer masterpiece almost melted before I could douse the threat.

Have you noticed that *age* is usually not mentioned in the same breath as *freedom*? We tease about it, send funny cards, dress in graveside clothing, and sometimes sink into a blue funk!

That is, unless you are sharing birthday cake with Arthur Winston. Arthur just retired from his job with the Los

Angeles transit at the age of one hundred. Yep, one hundred. Amazing, huh? And get this, he only missed one day of work in seventy-five years and that was the day of his wife's funeral. Truly amazing. Now that he's retiring, Arthur said he thought he'd use his new freedom to become a volunteer to help out old people.

Maybe Arthur could help me extinguish the candles on my cake this year. Art, here's a hint: bring a hydrant.

Speaking of freedom, have you heard about the ninety-five-year-old Japanese man who just set a record for his age group for running one hundred meters in 22.04 seconds? It takes me longer than that just to tie my shoes. He started participating in track events at the youthful age of sixty-five. Imagine getting started in a new career at the stage most folks are just getting comfy in their retirement swings. Even today he takes daily, hourlong walks. And the day he ran the race that put him on the record board, it was raining. He said he kept telling himself, *Just don't fall.*

Good advice. I say that to myself every morning when I get out of bed. *Steady, Patsy girl, what you have left has lost its bounce; so just don't fall.*

The resiliency of the human heart can last all our lives. Take, for instance, the one-hundred-year-old gentleman who was just awarded his master's of divinity degree. He actually earned it in 1951, but since blacks were not allowed to earn master's degrees from that school at that time, he had to wait more than five decades to receive what he earned. It was reported that at his long-awaited commencement ceremony, the crowd cheered when he walked up to receive his much-deserved honors. I wish I'd been there. I would have cheered too!

Years ago, he knew when he worked so faithfully week after week, and year after year, that man wouldn't give him recognition for his efforts—but he also knew he would have the personal satisfaction of a job well done. And that was something *no one* could take from him. That's freedom. Amazing freedom. I'm sorry he had to wait fifty-five years to be acknowledged, but I'm grateful he lived long enough to see folks come to their senses and acknowledge an honorable man's sterling intentions.

Speaking of sterling, tomorrow is my husband's birthday. Les is one year older than I am, which I really appreciate. I like living in a house where *something* in it is older than I am. (I don't count the ancient dust bunnies lurking in yonder closet.) Anyway, Les received a box of pasties as a gift from some friends. What's a pasty? Thank you for asking. It's a crust-encased meat and vegetable pie. Very yummy.

Les grew up in the Upper Peninsula of Michigan, where pasties were part of the weekly diet. Since a pasty made by a Patsy is way too redundant, his friends ordered him the real deal from his hometown of Calumet, Michigan.

So what does that have to do with the price of birthday

candles, you ask? Well, inside the box was a flier from the pasty company explaining that they are a business made up of assisted-living residents whose average age is eighty-four. Isn't that grand! Over eighty and still cookin'! That's what I'm talking about!

And while we're talking, let's not overlook a one-hundred-year-old New Yorker named Edward, who cooks up a weekly column for his hometown newspaper.

Or how about one-hundred-year-old Mahilda, who signed her name on the ticket to be a California gubernatorial candidate? She said she didn't like the way they were doing things. You go, girl.

While Mahilda is politicking, centenarian Inez from Minnesota had her first solo art show. Inez, you're proof it's never too late to brushstroke one's dreams into reality.

Lonnie, also a sprightly one hundred years old, continues, after years in the educational system as a teacher and principal, to make important contributions. Now she's a part of a Philanthropic Education Association, which owns a college and fosters the education of women. What a great legacy.

Speaking of legacy, we can't overlook Sadie and Gilbert, who lived to celebrate their eighty-first wedding anniversary. Imagine that. In a day and time when eighty-one weeks of marriage is thought to be something to celebrate, we have Sadie and Gilbert teaching us what endurance and commitment are all about.

And then there's Ray, who married at the age of 101. What an optimist! I wonder how old the ushers were?

Author Neenah Ellis wrote a book entitled *If I Live to Be 100.*[6] In this book, she includes interview excerpts she collected from people who are one hundred years old or older. Neenah said that during the interviews, she found herself mesmerized by their time-honored voices. While their voices were very different in tone and quality, they all were rich in personal history. Neenah encourages us to slow down and listen to others more closely, because, she says, "There is a universe in the sound of every voice."

Are there any old folks around you? I promise that many of them would love to chat with you. Just think what it would do for them . . . and you. Their voices will give you eyes into history. They'll help you experience by their first-hand accounts what you've only read about.

My grandmother, Thanie Elizabeth McEuen—"Mamaw" to us—almost made it to one hundred; she was ninety-seven and a half when she died. She witnessed the horse-and-buggy era to the first man on the moon. Talk about changing times. In her quivery voice, Mamaw told me how during her childhood they kept food underground to keep it cold and then eventually moved the food inside with the invention of the icebox. My grandmother was one of the last to give up her icebox for a new-fangled refrigerator. She wouldn't have changed even then, but there were no more home deliveries by ice men.

Mamaw was the sturdiest frail woman I'd ever met. She still had a red rinse put on her hair well into her nineties. I once asked her why she did that, and Mamaw replied, "Because I don't want to look old."

Bless her heart, when one endures that long, I say you can look any way you want. She wore what I thought were funny shoes and strange underwear and was a proper hankie-carrying, hat-wearing, Bible-toting lady through and through. (I can't imagine my grandchildren's description of me one day, with my spiky hairdo and my flashy jackets.)

And then there's Maria. Oh, didn't I tell you about her? She's our star. Maria is from Ecuador and is the oldest living person on earth, according to the *Guinness Book of World Records*. She lives with one of her daughters, eats unassisted, and still doesn't need eyeglasses. She's 116 years old.

You win, Maria, you win.

I read that there are seventy thousand centenarians in the United States alone. Amazing. I hope the accounts of these folks will add to your liberty regardless of how the years have stockpiled on your calendar. Remember, we never get so old that we can't try something we've never done before to keep ourselves current, fresh, and connected to those around us.

Today I'm trying to conquer the functioning of an iPod, a cell phone, and an updated laptop. I definitely don't learn as quickly as when my brain cells were on speaking terms with each other, but I'm determined to keep on keeping on until Jesus comes or I go, whichever comes first.

I want to be a pasty-making, race-running, degree-achieving, anniversary-celebrating, canvas-toting, chipper volunteer for as long as I can. I thank God for the brave folks who have gone before us to torch the way. Don't you just know that all these centenarians have days when they wonder if the effort's worth it? But may I say they are doing it for more than themselves, and so are we. The generation behind us is taking notes . . . may the stats on us be worth the read.

If we live to be one hundred, let's purpose together to not give up until our time here is done. Because of Christ, we have the freedom to live a full life. After all, who knows when the country will need well-seasoned women with funny underwear to run it?

I'm ready!

———

I'm ready to live a full life, Lord! I will keep loving and serving you for the rest of my life—even if I live to be one hundred.

Freedom for Eternity

Marilyn Meberg

> We, too, wait anxiously for that day when God will
> give us our full rights as his children, including the
> new bodies he has promised us. Now that we are
> saved, we eagerly look forward to this freedom.
>
> —Romans 8:23–24 NLT

This morning, my attention was captured by an article in the paper describing the many ways dogs can be trained to help their masters. One little dog named Melvin wore a harness that was attached to a harness worn by his owner, Mrs. B. Because of Mrs. B's diminishing mental capabilities, she would unwisely yield to the impulse to roam about the neighborhood. Whenever she stepped out of the house, Melvin would tug on his harness, which tugged on Mrs. B's harness. Melvin could then "tug" Mrs. B back home. Interestingly enough, she did not resist his tugging. When Mrs. B went to the mall with her daughter Lisa, Melvin worked especially hard because Mrs. B would frequently slip away. There was a beeper on Melvin's harness with a corresponding beeper in Lisa's purse. This system meant Mrs. B was never "lost," but her penchant for wandering off kept everyone on the alert.

Though I found the article fascinating, I was especially interested in Mrs. B's continual quest for freedom. What compelled her to try to give everyone the slip? What was she looking for that she did not already have? She was loved, well cared for, and physically secure. But in spite of her mental challenges, she had a clear desire to be free even from what was best for her.

The quest for freedom is not only characteristic of human beings but of the animal population as well. Let me tell you a few of my observations on that subject.

I live in an environment populated by gorgeously colored birds, egrets, several herons, a gazillion ducks, and two noisy but lovable geese. My property is on a man-made lake that connects to two other man-made lakes separated by stone bridges. My house is considered prime property because of its lake proximity. When I bought the house, I did not realize how enamored I would become with the wildlife flourishing in and around the lake. It is utterly engaging and satisfying to observe. But there is always a negative in paradise, and that negative is an industrious beaver whose intent is to chew down each tree that surrounds the lake. Freedom for him is living out his instinct to clear property of all trees and dam up all lakes. His freedom to chew and dam is encroaching upon the homeowners' freedom to preserve the trees and lakes.

Of all the animal wildlife offerings I'm experiencing, my favorite are the two squawking geese that love to eat bread from my hand (actually, from any hand). If I have not appeared at the iron fencing that protects my yard from their "bird packages," the two geese stand at the gate and squawk at me until I am made to realize their food schedule has been disrupted by my selfish pursuits in the house.

Pat Wenger, who lives down lake from me and is as attached to the geese as I am, burst into my house last week, announcing, "The geese are gone!" I had noticed the lack of squawking but had not gone outside to check on them. I realized then the quiet was unsettling. The two geese had indeed disappeared.

My next-door neighbor Bonnie had purchased those geese two years ago and released them to the lake herself. They have seemingly lived a contented life ever since. Because their wings were clipped, we knew they didn't fly anywhere. Did they meet with harm from someone? We were alarmed. Pat recruited Bonnie and then Dave across the street to begin a search. (At the time, I was housebound and reduced to anxious waiting.) Dave fishes the lake every evening while his two-year-old Ashland feeds the geese, so he, too, was emotionally invested in the whereabouts of "our geese."

It was nearly dark when the two geese spotted Bonnie, Dave, and Pat. They began squawking madly. They had somehow wandered up to another lake and found themselves surrounded by territorial ducks that did not welcome our geese. We wondered if they knew how to get back to their own lake. Bonnie tried to lure them with bread slices, but they would not follow. Instead, they chose to stay in a lake whose inhabitants were hostile to them.

Two days later, I heard their welcome squawking at my gate. The geese had come "home," bearing peck wounds on their necks and heads. Trying not to sound judgmental, I said to them as I fed them bread, "Why did you little morons leave the safety and security of this lake? What were you thinking? Did you think you would find a level of contentment beyond what you experience here daily? You have everything you could possibly want right here on this lake!"

I mutter the same questions of the prodigal son when I read his story in Luke 15. "What were you thinking? Did you actually think sinning wildly would be more satisfying than living morally? Did you ever think of the consequences when you dishonored your father, took your inheritance, and left your home?" Apparently the prodigal thought what he wanted more than anything in life was freedom. Freedom from what? The rules of his father's home? The rules of his culture that demanded right behavior and respect for one's heritage? Did he honestly consider respect and morality to be enslavement?

You will remember the prodigal son returned home in defeat. He'd squandered his inheritance and was reduced to poverty and homelessness. The freedom from all restraints was never realized. His need when he came home was greater than the need with which he left.

One of the reasons Jesus told the story of the prodigal was to illustrate the faithful love of God as seen in the example of the love of the prodigal's father. When the boy returned home, he did not receive the condemnation he expected and knew he deserved. Instead, his father threw a huge welcoming celebration. Perhaps it was then the boy knew and experienced real freedom.

All creation, human and animal, is driven by a desire for freedom. Why do you think that desire is so universal? What is the origin of this overwhelming quest?

I believe God wove into the inner fabric of his creation an insatiable desire to be free—free from bondage, free from domination, free from emotional hurt, free from physical suffering, and free from injustice, to cite only a few. Why did God create such a pervasive drive for freedom? Quite simply, that he might satisfy that drive. That we may experience then the very freedom from bondage, domination, emotional hurt, physical suffering, and injustice that accompanies every life experience we have on this imperfect planet. When God, and only God, satisfies this core need, we realize he is our only source for freedom and satisfaction. God's intention, then, was to create the awareness of need and then to satisfy that need.

I believe Jesus told the story of the prodigal not only to illustrate God's grace for his wayward creation but to underscore the reality that our need for freedom is met only as we return to the heart of our Father. As long as our focus is on other possible solutions for our freedom needs, we will be reduced to soul poverty. God knows that. We have to learn that. When we do figure it out, when we do understand the words of Jesus, who said, "You will know the truth, and truth will set you free" (John 8:32 NLT), we run back to the waiting arms of the Father. He knew all along we needed to come home. That's the truth that sets us free.

Though we as believers have returned to the heart of the Father, which we know was made possible by the death and resurrection of Jesus the Son, why then do we at times still feel a restlessness of spirit? Have we not believed well enough or committed ourselves deeply enough? When we know we are supposed to feel satisfied in our God-given freedom, how do we explain the fact that sometimes we aren't?

The answer to that question is simple: we don't have it all yet. There is a greater freedom to be experienced, and we won't know that full bathing of freedom until eternity. It is there we become whole in our new bodies and minds. It is there we live in spiritual completion. In the meantime, we wait for heavenly wholeness.

Romans 8:18–24 teaches us about our earthly yearning for eternal freedom:

Yet what we suffer now is nothing compared to the glory he will give us later. For all creation is waiting eagerly for that future day when God will reveal who his children really are. Against its will, everything on earth was subjected to God's curse. All creation anticipates the day when it will join God's children in glorious freedom from death and decay. For we know that all creation has been groaning as in the pains of childbirth right up to the present time. And even we Christians, although we have the Holy Spirit within us as a foretaste of future glory, also groan to be released from pain and suffering. We, too, wait anxiously for that day when God will give us our full rights as his children, including the new bodies he has promised us. Now that we are saved, we eagerly look forward to this freedom. (NLT)

God has provided everything we need to live our lives on this earth. But in the living here, we know there's more to come. We don't need to feel guilty when we groan for our eternal freedom.

———

Father God, how I long for the freedom and wholeness
I will experience in heaven! Help me to be patient today,
knowing that the best is yet to come.

Free Indeed

Mary Graham

Therefore if the Son makes you free,
you shall be free indeed.

—John 8:36 NKJV

*I*t was my first trip to the former Soviet Union. I was traveling with five friends in an effort to help establish ministry on campuses. It was the early 1980s, and the Communist government had a very tight rein on Westerners entering the country. The Soviet citizens were held in an atheistic grip, and our interactions with them were regarded suspiciously, so we were very careful.

Our first stop was Leningrad, where we spent a wonderful, adventurous week with several university students whom we met casually and became fast friends with. They were studying English and were eager for us to help them with their language skills. In the course of conversation, we talked about faith and saw their hearts respond. By the time we left their city, it was with a commitment to return.

Because our week had been amazing, we felt energized as we headed to our second city, Kiev, in the Ukraine, which had the reputation of being much freer, more open to Americans, and more advanced. The train trip to cross the country was a bit more challenging than we'd anticipated, but I was happy and eager to find English-speaking students and strike up great conversations.

But it was Saturday night. We needed to find the hotel, have dinner, get a good night's rest, and decide what to do on Sunday morning. From the train station, we took a taxi to the hotel. One of my friends, Patty, checked us all in. At the desk, she turned to us and asked for passports and visas. I handed her my passport but couldn't seem to find the visa that gave me permission to be in the country. I looked. And looked. And looked again.

Casually, and with innocence coming from sheer ignorance, I smiled and said, "I'm so sorry. I've lost my visa." The entire room got very quiet. And *very* cold. No one said anything or moved a muscle. I smiled and tried to explain. I smiled again and was apologetic. I needed the guard to understand I brought a visa, but it was now missing. She needed me to understand I was in very serious trouble. Neither of us understood the other.

Finally, in desperation, I asked a friend to go through my

bags. She found no visa. I went to the woman, dressed in a uniform, standing behind the desk looking very intimidating and with no trace of kindness. In my best and slowest English, I said as kindly as I could, "I'm very sorry, ma'am. I cannot find my visa." She looked me square in the face and said slowly and with sheer determination, "It is not possible. You cannot be in our country *vitout* your *wesa*." Her English wasn't perfect, but there was no mistaking what she communicated.

This exchange continued for a few more minutes: my explanation, followed by her insistence. It was a standoff. Ultimately, I understood my good intentions were no match for her intolerance. She took me in a room separating me from my friends. At a table in the room sat three armed guards. She stood in front of them, facing me. Again she said, "It is not possible. You cannot be in our country *vitout* your *wesa*"—as if those were the only words she knew.

I was as scared as I've ever been in my life. Finally, I relented. "I'll just go home. I'll go to the airport and fly straight home. Without my friends. It's not a problem."

"It is not possible! You cannot leave our country *vitout* your *wesa*!" she screamed. New sentence, same forceful delivery. And I promise you, when she said those words, she actually got bigger. Then she added new data. "Ve tink you did not lose your *wesa*. Ve tink you *gave* your *wesa* to a Soviet citizen. Perhaps you *sold* your *wesa* to a Soviet citizen. We must send you to Moscow."

No, thank you. This was the Cold War, and I shuddered to think I'd be a prisoner of it. I was naive enough to actually utter the words, "I cannot go to Moscow. It is not on my itinerary." I don't know how much English she really understood but enough to know that was a stupid, ridiculous statement. She said nothing.

Being a Saturday night, there was nothing more they could do. They took me to my room and told me to stay there until they came for me on Sunday morning. My friend Patty was in the room, and we prayed. Amazingly, I was flooded with a sense of freedom. Freedom that comes from knowing God is sovereign and nothing could happen to me apart from his protection and provision. He was in control. While I didn't feel it at the moment, it was my reality and I knew it. When we finished praying, I opened my bag—and on the top was my visa. I thought I was hallucinating. I didn't even touch it for a couple of seconds. Two people besides me had searched that bag, *and every bag.* Yet there it lay right on top. Patty and I stared for a moment, silently . . . then we praised God, cried, and laughed.

Patty went with me back to the lobby. I waved the visa in the air and announced to the saber-rattling general, "I found my visa." She barely blinked, but that frayed, faded piece of paper was my ticket to freedom. It enabled me to stay in the country and provided freedom to return home a few days later.

As a citizen of the United States, I've always lived with freedom. Freedom to come and go as I please, freedom to change my mind and plans, freedom to express my opinions, freedom to differ, freedom to choose, freedom to be. Freedom opens doors and creates opportunity. Having your freedom removed or limited, even for a moment in time, is frightful and intimidating. I not only remember that moment when my freedom was threatened, but I haven't forgotten how it felt.

A few years after my incident in Kiev, I was in Leningrad doing ministry there among students who, by now, were friends. Patty and I were at the train station saying good-bye and preparing to board a train to Helsinki for our flight to America. Misha, a student we knew, came running up to us and breathlessly cried out, "The wall in Germany has come down!" We knew that was impossible, so we tried to extract the real information he'd heard.

He explained he'd been listening to BBC News on his shortwave radio (which was strictly forbidden in those days) and that the wall between the East and the West had come down and people were moving freely from one side to the other. It sounded like a fairy tale for such a world-changing event to have happened in such a short time.

That wall had been erected in 1949 to divide East Berlin and West Berlin; ultimately, the Eastern part of Europe was occupied by the Soviets. The Berlin Wall became a symbol of the lack of freedom. In Western Europe, people were free to make choices of their own. In Eastern Europe, however, they were held hostage to a heavy-handed, belligerent government. The contrast was apparent in every way.

We all wanted the wall removed. After all, it is heart-breaking to see innocent people being held captive by a tyrannical government. Everyone longed for freedom. And now Misha was saying our prayers had been answered? How could it be as simple as that? Patty said, "Misha, your English is not that good. You must have misunderstood."

We were both very sure about that . . . until our train pulled into the station in Finland. Everywhere we looked in this modern, Western culture, only a few hours from the barbed-wire border of the Soviet Union, the news was plastered: THE WALL COMES DOWN.

The surreal experience of walking through that train station and seeing the news of the Berlin Wall coming down is one of the highlights of my life that I will never forget. Eastern Europe was free, and the prayers of believers everywhere had helped significantly in that process. I was overwhelmed with emotion and can still be when I think back to those first moments.

Since those days, freedom has taken on new meaning for me, to be sure. But the older I get, I'm more aware that political and economic freedom is not the answer to the cry of our hearts. The freedom for which we long is really much deeper, more elusive, and harder won than that.

The freedom for which we were created is not freedom from a tyrannical political system; it's freedom from ourselves—freedom from our own selfishness, pettiness, limitations, fear, and sin. It's freedom that comes from knowing God is always in control.

That's why Jesus said, "Therefore if the Son makes you free, you shall be free *indeed*" (John 8:36 NKJV; emphasis added).

God, today—and for the rest of my life—allow me to experience your amazing freedom.

Notes

1. Dayna Curry, Heather Mercer, and Stacy Mattingly, *Prisoners of Hope: The Story of Our Captivity and Freedom in Afghanistan* (Colorado Springs: Waterbrook, 2003).

2. Ney Bailey, *Faith Is Not a Feeling: Choosing to Take God at His Word*, 3rd ed. (Colorado Springs: Waterbrook, 2002).

3. Wolfgang Puck, *Modern French Cooking for the American Kitchen* (Boston, MA: Houghton Mifflin, 1981), xv.

4. Chris Maynard and Bill Sheller, *Manifold Destiny: The One! The Only! Guide to Cooking on Your Car Engine!* (New York, Villard, 1989).

5. Will and Ariel Durant, *The Story of Civilization*, 11 vols. (New York: Simon & Schuster, 1954).

6. Neenah Ellis, *If I Live to Be 100: Lessons from the Centenarians* (New York: Three Rivers Press, 2004).